Game Programming
for Artists

Game Programming
for Artists

by
Jarryd Huntley
and
Hanna Brady

CRC Press
Taylor & Francis Group
Boca Raton London New York

CRC Press is an imprint of the
Taylor & Francis Group, an **informa** business
AN A K PETERS BOOK

CRC Press
Taylor & Francis Group
6000 Broken Sound Parkway NW, Suite 300
Boca Raton, FL 33487-2742

© 2018 by Taylor & Francis Group, LLC
CRC Press is an imprint of Taylor & Francis Group, an Informa business

No claim to original U.S. Government works

Printed on acid-free paper

International Standard Book Number-13: 978-1-1381-0613-0 (Hardback)
International Standard Book Number-13: 978-1-1386-2646-1 (Paperback)

Library of Congress Cataloging-in-Publication Data

Names: Huntley, Jarryd, author. | Brady, Hanna, 1987- author.
Title: Game programming for artists / Jarryd Huntley and Hanna Brady.
Description: Boca Raton : CRC Press, [2018] | Includes bibliographical
references.
Identifiers: LCCN 2017016518 | ISBN 9781138106130 (hardback : acid-free paper)
| ISBN 9781138626461 (pbk. : acid-free paper)
Subjects: LCSH: Computer games--Programming. | Computer games--Design.
Classification: LCC QA76.76.C672 .H86 2018 | DDC 794.8/1526--dc23
LC record available at https://lccn.loc.gov/2017016518

Visit the Taylor & Francis Web site at
http://www.taylorandfrancis.com

and the CRC Press Web site at
http://www.crcpress.com

Contents

Foreword

PEOPLE HAVE ASKED ME—WHY the heck should an artist learn to code? Shouldn't they just focus on art? Well, they shouldn't give up their art, that's for sure, but when it comes to learning to code, there are so many great reasons to do it! First, there's independence. If you're an artist who can code, you can basically make 90% of a video game on your own. Second, even if you don't go so far as to work on a game solo, technical artists are a burgeoning and yet surprisingly rare section of the game industry, who bridge the gap between multiple disciplines, making art more efficient in-game, while also shaping tools that help artists do their jobs better. It's a job that's in high demand.

But even more basic than that, understanding how code works, indeed how games work, will help you integrate better with any game team you come across. As creative director for my company, I'm often pushing at the limits of what we can do with our games. Does the engine support this? Can I do this thing with our scripting language? The most annoying question a designer, artist, or other noncode person can ask a programmer is "but can't you just ...?" If you don't know what can be done in the game, these kinds of questions wind up slowing down the development of your game.

If you learn even some basic programming, you'll better understand what the game you're making is capable of, and how it's set up from the very start. You'll also understand the ways to make your art in more efficient ways. Is this work better implemented as a full sprite sheet, with all animation frames displayed for each character, or are some frames reused, so that you should only include the unique ones and call them when needed by specific animations?

As you begin the process of learning to code, these questions will begin to pop up in front of you left and right—and as you answer them, the entire game development pipeline will become easier, more efficient, and more enjoyable, because you'll get to spend more time making art and less time on the process.

So if you're looking at this book, congratulations on taking that first step. Artists like you with the desire to learn code are in short supply. But you are so, so necessary, and you're the kind of artist that project leads are looking for. And as you learn, remember to flex these coding muscles occasionally! Join a game jam as a coder, and see what happens! You'll learn massive amounts in the process, as there's simply no replacement for experience.

So take this ride with Jarryd and Hanna, two educators who want nothing more than to get you on the right track. Have fun, learn well, and make great games!

Brandon Sheffield
Necrosoft Games

Introduction

WELCOME!

Thanks for picking up *Game Programming for Artists*!

We wrote this book for people in the arts who are interested in learning about programming for the first time. Maybe you're a digital artist who is ready to dive into the code. Maybe you're used to working in a physical medium and you're curious about the world of ones and zeroes. Maybe you're just looking for an approach to learning some game programming that's a bit more conversational than most computer science textbooks. Quite possibly you're something else entirely. Wherever you're coming from, we're glad you're here.

One of the great things about working on games is getting to work with a lot of different disciples—whether that's in the form of a team with diverse skills or it's you learning a lot of different tools. Video games pull from all sorts of other areas: art, psychology, music, design, computer science, and more.

Jarryd wears a lot of hats. He's an indie game developer, a community organizer, a programming instructor, and more. In college, he majored in computer science and played in a rock band. Now he lives in the world of games, too!

Which is part of why game makers come from a lot of different backgrounds (check out our author sidebars for examples). Really, we wanted to write this book to encourage that particular aspect of games. You don't need to be a computer science major to do a bit of programming and we wanted to demystify what a programmer is up to. You can accomplish a lot with a little here.

This book isn't going to turn you into an expert programmer. Nothing's that simple, right? But it will give you the basics of programming—enough to start making simple games. It should also give you confidence in continuing to pursue making video games—whether that's better communication with a programmer, improving your own programming skills, or just a clearer idea of what it's going to take to make your dream game real. And finally, it should help you start to think like a programmer—which is useful when you are trying to talk to a computer.

Hanna writes stories for games. She started out as a technophobic English major. She surprised herself and everyone who knew her when she made her way into video games, but she loves it here.

We're going to get into what exactly is in the book in just a moment here, but before we do…

We want to wish you persistence and curiosity as you pursue learning how to program for games. Everyone starts at the beginning and we're cheering for you. May your code be bug free and your players happy!

The Nitty Gritty

So, what are you going to find in this book?

Game Programming for Artists is divided into three sections. The first is an "Introduction to Programming." Here you'll find answers to the basics: What's a programming language? How does a computer read it? You'll find simple programming concepts, how to write and apply them in code, along with suggestions for starting to think like a programmer.

The second section is an "Introduction to Game Engines." Here you'll find answers to questions like: What's a game engine? Why do I use a game engine? What sort of things does a game engine do? Which one should I use? We also go through how game engines run in detail—so you have a holistic idea of how a game goes from code to the screen.

Then we have the "recipes" chapters. These consist of different programming concepts divided into *recipes*. We'll introduce a few more programming concepts—building on the Introduction to Programming. We'll also do things like show you how to program a 2D platformer and simple AIs.

Finally, you'll find a glossary of game jargon and some notes on different tools to help you build your games at the end.

Ready? Let's get started!

CHAPTER 1

Introduction to Programming

CLICHÉ AS IT IS, there's still nowhere better to begin than at the beginning. We're going to assume you've never tinkered with writing a program before. For many of you, this may not actually be true. Today, there are so many ways to try your hand at learning to code that sometimes it's the overabundance of information that stops us rather than the scarcity.

Part of what we're trying to do is to give you a practical foundation for programming whatever projects you want to create. Another part is to give you the critical knowledge that will help you choose the tools and skills best suited to your foray into game programming.

By the end of this section, you should have a solid understanding of what a programming language is and the most basic tools they provide to us. You'll have the beginning of a programming vocabulary and be familiar with the pieces that can make up a program.

But first! A few thoughts to keep in the background as we go...

A PROGRAM BY ANY OTHER NAME

Before we get into the meat (or tofu) of this section, let's look at what a program can be. You may think you've never followed a program before, but we'd wager you have.

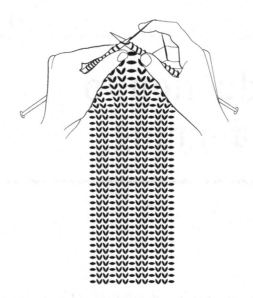

FIGURE 1.1   When you are knitting, you can accomplish a lot with only two stitches: knit and purl. A bit like binary!

Have you ever followed a knitting (Figure 1.1) or cross-stitch pattern? Learned a dance? How about reading a sheet of music or following a set of instructions for putting together a piece of furniture?

You've guessed it, right? We can consider any of those programs.

At its most basic level, a program is a series of instructions to be followed in order. So, a step chart or a series of movements described verbally is a set of instructions we follow in order to produce a waltz or a cha-cha. A sheet of music tells us which piano keys to press in order to reproduce a specific composition. A computer program is the same idea.

We write a series of commands, and that's our program. The commands are instructions the computer knows how to perform.

Like any of the everyday or artistic *programs* mentioned above, there are vocabulary conventions that go with successfully communicating a set of instructions. Whether it's simply giving the instructions in an expected order—from left to right, or right to left—or including specific contextual information—like a treble clef in music—the information surrounding the instructions make them understandable. You'll need to learn programming's conventions and rules in order to successfully communicate with a computer. Knowing how to read a program and being able to write your own program takes practice and time.

You have to learn the language. Don't worry. It's not as hard as it sounds.

COMPUTERS ARE DUMB...

This may seem funny at first, but it's important to keep in mind as we learn this new language.

Why does it matter, you ask?

Because when we say *computers are dumb*, we actually mean *computers are really dumb*. They don't understand pictures or sentences or what it means when we get frustrated and yell at the screen (even if sometimes that's what seems to work).

Computers only understand two things: ones and zeroes. On and off. True and false.

That's it. This is called binary. Binary means one of the two states, as in the above-mentioned examples. So how does the computer understand how to check your spelling? How does your phone understand dictation?

These more advanced features are built on top of many layers of programs and those layers eventually come down to binary. That's the only *language* the computer actually understands.

Keep this in mind because the computer will always happily go about doing exactly what we told it to do. Nothing more and nothing less. If we accidentally tell the computer to open 10,000 instances of one document, that's exactly what it will try to do. The computer will heartlessly delete folders or replicate them forever if we give it the right (or wrong) commands. The computer is unaware of what it's doing. It's always just following the instructions we gave it.

Because of this, we must be diligent in making sure we tell the computer exactly what we want it to do. Typos are enough to derail a computer program and give you an error. But on top of that, small mistakes can add up into nasty complex bugs.

...AND PROGRAMMERS ARE LAZY

You'll learn to love this one. We don't mean that programmers live inactive lifestyles or that they're unhealthy. What we mean is that when it comes to programming, programmers work to become more and more efficient.

Say we task a programmer with solving a problem. Say that either technique A or technique B will accomplish the work. If both techniques are equally effective, but B is a hair easier or faster to implement—11 out of 10 programmers will choose B. Yes, we're being flippant here, but the point is that all programmers learn tricks to become more efficient. And as they (and you!) attack new, larger, and more complicated problems, these skills in laziness-efficiency will pay off.

DON'T FEAR THE MATH

As you opened this book, you might have thought, *I'm not good at math* or *I don't like math* and how are you supposed to be a programmer if that's true? We'll start by saying: that's a loaded question. But let's work with it a moment.

So, we actually believe most people are better at math than they think. Math tends to be presented and tested in a school setting through standardized tests. Which isn't always the best gauge of anyone's understanding of mathematics. Indie game programming is a very different setting from the classroom. As long as your math works, nobody cares what it looks like. Obviously, there may be certain advantages to doing something one way or another. But when it comes down to it, as long as you've solved the problem, you've solved the problem.

Now, game programming does require an understanding of mathematics. Basic arithmetic is the minimum. Beyond that, an understanding of geometry and basic algebra is useful. If you're familiar with higher math, you'll be prepared to take on

> If you're concerned that your solution is not the *prettiest* or most *elegant*, don't worry about it! Games hold some of the most *interesting* code— thrown together to meet deadlines and to get things working. If you get the chance to come back and tidy things up, that's great. But frequently the messy code sticks around. Often, as long as it's functional, nobody's the wiser.

different types of problems; but beyond that, it doesn't necessarily make you better equipped for programming.

Here's the thing about math and programming: You don't need to do the math.

Say what?

The purpose of computers themselves is to solve complex computations for us. Our understanding of math comes into play when figuring out how best to describe or express those problems to the computer. We don't need to *show our work* or manually solve for x, and we don't need to find the derivative. That's the computer's job. But if we know how to frame the problem and know what we're asking the computer to do, it'll make things easier.

Onward!

Moving forward we want you to keep these things in mind: programs are common in everyday life, computers are dumb, remember to be lazy, and you can do the math!

Let's get back to learning about this new type of language.

PROGRAMMING LANGUAGES

So we've gotten into what programs are and can be. We've got some advice about approaching this work as a programmer and we're looking forward to programming our own games.

Before we get to using the languages, it's worth knowing a bit more about them. We're going to look at programming languages in general and some of the ones that are popular for programming games.

All computer programs are written in programming languages. There are hundreds of programming languages. All these languages have strengths, weaknesses, and cases in which they are most useful. Additionally, all programming languages can be grouped into different classes and families—making it easier to distinguish what language will be most useful for the project or field you are tackling.

We have two main varieties of programming languages: interpreted and compiled. As you've probably guessed, they've each got advantages and disadvantages. This won't affect how you approach programming a ton, but these differences are good information to have in the back of your head.

Interpreted Languages

So let's begin by thinking about programming languages as spoken languages and imagine we have a professional translator: Luiza. Luiza's job is to help native Portuguese speakers communicate with people who don't speak the language. Imagine she is following a client around. She's able to translate conversations as they happen, just a bit slower than real time. As the conversation progresses, she translates each sentence as it comes. This is similar to how an interpreted language works—hence the name. The computer reads in the program's files, interprets the data, and produces a result. Or runs the program (Figure 1.2).

The advantage is that it's a simple process: the program is read in and a result is produced.

Programs written in interpreted languages are also more portable because they use an *interpreter*. An interpreter in this case is a specific

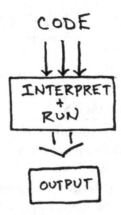

FIGURE 1.2   The flow for an interpreted programming language.

program that is used to interpret another program. An example would be a web browser: You can write using an interpreted language, like JavaScript, and have it run in all sorts of different web browsers, on different operating systems and devices.

The downside is a slower running speed. There may be specific optimizations or shortcuts in place that the computer could perform, but since it doesn't know what's coming next in the program, it can't take advantage of them.

Compiled Languages

On the other hand, we have compiled languages. Let's bring back Luiza the imaginary translator. This time her client has asked her to translate a large stack of documents from Portuguese to English. As she's working through translating the pile, she becomes more familiar with the phrases and vocabulary that repeat in the documents. She can begin to predict what's coming next. And she'll become more and more efficient in translating.

Once she's done with the translation, Luiza no longer needs to be involved in the conversation. An English speaker can read the documents without pause or assistance, and they can read them at full speed because all the work has already been done.

This is similar to how a compiled programming language works. The computer runs through all the code, optimizes it, and translates it into a special set of instructions in machine code (Figure 1.3). Machine code is not designed to be read by humans. Instead, it's a specific language optimized for the processor in your computer to read as fast as possible.

FIGURE 1.3   The flow for a compiled programming language.

Using a game engine, no further translation work is needed and the processor can run it immediately. This is where we get a lot of our speed advantages with a compiled language.

You won't encounter the disadvantages of using a compiled language directly, but it's good to be aware of them. Since a compiled programming language is designed to run directly on the processor (CPU), the compiler needs to be designed to handle many types of processor. This means that if we compile a program for one processor, it won't work on another type. The same is often true with operating systems. So, we need to recompile our programs for each variation of processor and operating system we want to support. Also, as new processors are developed a compiler needs to be modified before we can write programs for them.

Syntax

Each family of programming languages and each language has its own syntax and rules. As with spoken languages, once you learn a first programming language you'll have an easier time learning a second from the same family. Along with that, once you learn one programming language—from any family—learning any other programming language becomes much easier. The process changes from learning all the rules and vocabulary from scratch to picking up the subtle and not-so-subtle differences from the other languages you know.

Again, as with spoken languages, different programming languages can be used to express the same ideas. Each programming language has its own specific rules, so the ideas will be constructed differently, some more or less efficiently, but they will all get the job done.

> In most human languages, syntax is the proper or elegant arrangement of words into sentences. In programming languages, syntax refers to the rules of writing code in such a way that it's understood by the computer. Syntax is the code for writing code.

C# and C++

In this book, we'll be focusing on the programming languages: C# (read as *C sharp*), We'll briefly look at C++ (read as *C plus plus*), and JavaScript.

C#, C++, and JavaScript come from the same family of programming languages, referred to as *C-like Programming Languages*. These are popular languages for general programming and for game programming.

C# is newer and could be considered a descendent from C++. They share a lot of the same syntax, rules, and feel. They are, however, used in fairly different ways.

C++ is an extremely powerful programming language. It gives you virtually unlimited options. Very few programming languages can match C++ in its speed and power. The main downside to C++ is its complexity. It can be a relatively difficult programming language to learn. Along with all that power comes a great deal of syntax, many considerations to keep in mind, and techniques to master. *Unreal*, *id Tech*, *Source* and *Crytek* are all game engines built in C++.

JavaScript

JavaScript is one of the most popular programming languages, and it shares some syntax with C# and C++. The big difference between the two is that JavaScript is a web programming language, and its interpreters are built into your browser. When programming games for the web, JavaScript is your first and best option.

It's also possible to use JavaScript to write games and programs as apps for mobile devices and even desktop computers. In order to do this though, we have to trick JavaScript into thinking it's working on the web. We do this by using "wrappers." Wrappers are like small specialized web browsers trimmed down to the bare minimum. You could think of them like a stripped down version of Google Chrome or Safari. Wrappers essentially act as interpreters, allowing the program to run on a mobile device and providing the illusion that it is a normal app.

COMMON PROGRAMMING CONSTRUCTS (OR BUILDING BLOCKS)

All programming languages have a certain set of tools built into them. These sets are fairly standardized across languages and families. We refer to them as constructs. After a quick note on formatting, we'll get into the most common programming constructs—what they are and how to use them.

Formatting

All programming languages have punctuation, formatting, and keywords that make them unique. When beginning to learn a language, it's best to start by checking out the syntax or writing rules. These are guidelines that will ensure you have clean, error-free code.

Generally, programming one line of code equates to one command. Eventually, as we learn more advanced commands, that may become less true. But for the moment, think of one line of code as one command. Another way to think about it is to consider each line of code as a simple sentence. Each sentence tells the computer to complete one task.

Each programming language has a way to signify when a line of code is complete. There is no limit on how long or short a line of code should be. Remember, computers are dumb.

Since there is no limit to how long a line of code can or should be, we need to make sure we have some way of telling the computer where the end of a line of code is. Thinking about it as a sentence in English: we need a period.

In C#, C++, and JavaScript, it's all the same. We end a line of code with a semicolon(;). We'll use these at the end of each line of code to say we're done and ready to give the computer another command.

Let's look at the following line of code:

```
Actor playerCharacter = new Actor(15, "PlayerOne");
```

Even though we have no idea what it's doing yet, we can tell where it ends. Recognizing where a line of code ends is an important skill in learning how to read and write code.

When a computer runs our program, it will begin with the top line of code. After completing that first line (stopping at a semicolon), it will move on to the next. Programs always run from the top most line of code to the bottom and final line.

Another important piece of punctuation are curly braces ({ }). These are used to separate sections of code. You could compare it to paragraphs in English. We use an opening curly brace ({) to start a new section of code, called a code block, and a closing curly brace (}) to end a section. The section in between the curly braces is called the body. The contents of each code block should be indented one level further in than the curly braces like so:

```
{← Opening curly brace
      //Body
      //One or more lines of code go here
} ← Closing curly brace
```

We'll explore using this format to define different types of commands in programming in the coming sections of this chapter. Often code blocks are tied to a command. Commands usually have one line of code declaring the command, and then a code block to define the body of the command. You're going to see this pattern over and over.

The body of a code block can contain one or more lines of code, or even more code blocks. If a code block contains another code block, the inner block is nested inside the first. Nesting is a tool we'll explore more in depth later. It can help us to organize, group, and arrange code based on functionality. This is what it looks like:

```
{← The start of the outer code block
      //A line of code
      //Another line of code
      {← The start of the nested (or inner) code block
            //More lines of code
            //Notice how these lines are indented
            //one level more than the curly braces
      }

}
```

Technically, we can nest as many times as we want—nesting code block within code block indefinitely. However, nesting too many times becomes impractical and will negatively impact our code's readability.

We're going to talk about one more piece of formatting before moving on to the constructs. Often, as you are programming, you'll want a way to take notes. Whether you're writing reminders to yourself or documentation for other programmers, it's useful to be able to leave a note in the code. That's what comments are for.

There are two main types of comments: single line comments and block comments. Single line comments are for quick notes and—you guessed it!—must be written as a single line. They use the following format:

Readability, when it comes to code, is how easy it is for a person to read your code. You can improve your readability in a number of ways, and we'll touch on some throughout the book.

```
// Anything following two slashes is the comment.
```

Now remaining on a single line is not always practical, which is why we have block comments.

Block comments work in the same way as single line comments, letting us leave notes and reminders inside the code, but we can use as many lines as we need! Like a code block, they have starting and ending symbols:

```
/* ← This starts the block comment

    The body of the block comment is here.
    We can use as many lines of code as we want.
    Anything goes here!

*/ ← This ends the block comment
```

Comments are quite useful. But too many will decrease the readability of our code. To avoid that, here are two things to keep in mind: First, write comments for other programmers. Comments aren't the place to explain how something works from the ground up, because anyone looking at the code (other programmers and developers) should already have an idea of what they are looking at. Second, go easy on the comments. Excessive comments bury the actual code. That makes it harder to read and harder to maintain.

Comments are also useful when we want to quickly enable or disable a line or lines of code in order to test something. If we have a line of code we'd like to try removing, we can quickly add forward slashes to the beginning of a line. The code becomes a comment and it is disabled.

To reverse the process, we just remove those forward slashes. It'll save you from copying and pasting your code around or risking the introduction of errors by retyping the code.

Now that we have some formatting under our belt, it's time to look at our programming constructs. As you read, note the placement and use of the semicolons and the curly braces in the examples.

There are dozens of rules for formatting each different language. We'll get into more rules for C# later. But for now, we'll just reiterate that one way this is different from an ordinary sentence is that if your formatting is off even a little, the program will break. If you are programming your own game, plan on spending time combing through your code for that one syntax error, and remember that everyone will be doing that at one point or another.

Variables

Now that we know how the computer is accepting instructions and how to tell the computer when an instruction is done, what's next? All programming comes down to the computer taking values, changing values, and reporting the results.

We need to tell the computer where and how to store those values before we do anything with them. In programming, we store information (data, values, etc...) in variables.

You can think of variables as a kind of storage container. When we need to store information we grab a new container, mention what type of information or item we will be storing inside, give it a name, and then put the information inside.

From there we can return to, retrieve, change, or remove the information altogether. So long as we use the correct name for the container, the computer will know what we're talking about.

As an example, perhaps at the beginning of your game, you want players to start with zero points. You might name a variable `numberOfPoints` and fill it with a number. Because this variable will always be represented by a number, we use `int` at the beginning (short for integer). That's defining what sort of data type `numberOfPoints` will be. The next section is on data types, but before we get there, let's take a look at this variable example. This is how that would appear in code:

```
int numberOfPoints = 0;
```

That's a pretty simple example. Remember that you can store more than numbers in variables. In fact, you can store all sorts of data…

Data Types

We won't get into all the specifics of data types at this point, but we'll cover the basics. We've learned how to store information in variables; data types are the defined categories of information we can store in variables. There are a number of different data types, each for storing specific kinds of information. Rather than explore them all in detail, we'll just cover the three main varieties:

> It can be strange to start thinking about things as common as the alphabet and simple sentences as pieces of data. But the individual letters of the alphabet are considered characters and when we write a sentence, it's a sequence of characters. That sequence of characters is a string.

Numeric

Numeric data types are designed to store different kinds of numbers. Some are designed to hold large numbers, some for smaller numbers, and others for numbers with decimal points. For now, we'll just stick to using the numeric data type int. When you see int, just remember the variable is holding some type of number.

String and Character

These kinds of data types are designed to hold characters—as in letters, symbols, or glyphs. Single characters can be stored in a variable by themselves. We can also store multiple characters in order, this is called a string. We can use strings to represent sentences, paragraphs, or any type of ordered character data.

Boolean

This is the specific type of variable designed to hold booleans, which are values that are either true or false. We can use them to represent whether a scenario is true or false, whether something is on or off, whether something is present or not. One of the benefits of a boolean is that when we begin talking about conditions later in this chapter, we can put a boolean value directly into a condition.

> Although there are differences in syntax between C#, C++, and JavaScript, all the examples in this chapter are the same in all three languages!

One final note on variables before we move on: Variables only exist in the code block where they are defined, and inside any nested code blocks. Once the code block where the variable is defined has completed, the variables will cease to exist. As long as we're in the same code block, we can access, modify, and read the variable. The concept of how long a variable lasts and where it is available is called variable scope.

Ready to start playing with those variables?

Operators

Now that we have information in the form of variables, we need to know how to manipulate and change it. In order to modify variables, adjust the output, or perform any sort of action, we'll be using operations. Operations each have a specific symbol and they perform a specific action. You're already familiar with a number of the most common operators in programming: addition (+), subtraction (−), multiplication (*), and division (/). The equals sign (=) is used a little bit differently and we'll also be talking about modulus (%) which you may be unfamiliar with.

We use operators on specific data: often stored in variables, just like in mathematics. The main difference being that we have the computer doing the work for us, based on which operators we pick and the values we provide it to work on. Most programming languages share the majority of operators. So, if you learn how operators work in one language, they'll work similarly in other programming languages—even if they use a different format.

Let's translate the operators you're familiar with into code, so that you can get used to reading them.

Addition (+)
Addition is the same operator you are familiar with from basic arithmetic. We can use it to add two variables together or to add a number to a variable.

```
int score = oldScore + 20;
```

Subtraction (−)
Like addition, subtraction is the operator you're already familiar with. We can use it to subtract one value from another.

```
int score = oldScore - 40;
```

Multiplication (*)
We can use the multiplication operator to perform multiplication on two values and get the result.

```
int score = oldScore * 20;
```

Division (/)
We can get the result of a division between two values by using this operator.

```
int score = oldScore / 20;
```

Modulus (%)
This operator may be new to you, but it's probably not as unfamiliar as you might think. Basically, the modulus operator performs division, but returns the remainder to us: the parts left over.

Imagine we have a room with 20 seats and we have 24 people attending our event. If we divide 20 seats by 24 people, we get 1. Meaning, we could fill the room entirely once. But say we wanted to know how many people still needed seats. If we perform 24 % 20 instead, then the remainder portion (4 in this case) is returned.

Another use case for modulus is to determine if a number is odd or even. Yes, we know that it seems like a computer should already know if a number is odd or even. But remember computers are dumb. So, to determine if a number is odd or even, we perform modulus two (%2) on a number. Dividing an even number will give us the remainder zero, while an odd will return a 1.

```
int remainder = 8 % 3;
```

Assignment (=)
We talked about variables. This is the operator we use to assign values to variables. Here's the basic format for storing variable data. Note our assignment operator.

```
datatype variableName = value;
```

When we have a single equals sign, it acts as an assignment operator. You can think about it as a middle point, separating the information on the right side and on the left. This will always put the value on the right side of the = into the left side. And the information on the right side must match the data type defined on the left.

Now, what if we want to update a value or change it? We can use nearly the same format we did when we created the variable. The only difference being that we don't have to define the data type. The data type of a variable should not change. So! We can write:

```
variableName = newValue;
```

And set a new value for our variable.

When we want to retrieve the value stored in a variable, we ask for it by using the variable's name. When the computer sees the variable name alone, without the following equals sign, it knows we are asking for the value. We don't need to keep exact track of what's in the variable. That's the computer's job.

Comparators

We're going to look at one more kind of operator: comparators. Now that we know how to create and track variables, we will want a way to compare them. That way we can start to make decisions, answer questions, and change our outcomes based on the differences in variable values.

The most common comparison is the equals comparison. A single equals sign (=) is used as our assignment operator, so in order to compare values we use two equals signs (==). As follows:

```
variableName == compareTo
```

Other comparators include: greater than (>), less than (<), greater than or equal to (>=), less than or equal to (<=), and not equal to (!=).

Neither = nor == is used precisely the way we would in ordinary arithmetic. = is used to assign a value. In other words, it is used to declare that a variable has a certain value. == on the other hand is used to check whether the two sides of the equation are equal. To compare them to one another.

We can compare a variable to a number of different things. We can compare it to a value. We can compare it to another variable. We can compare it to a certain scenario based on input received from the user. We have a lot of flexibility here that will come in handy as we write our programs.

Increment and Decrement (++ *and* --)

When we are dealing with a numerical value in a game, it's quite common to want to increase or decrease that number by one. For example, if a player finds a crystal and collects it, their total number of `crystalsCollected` goes up by one. Another scenario: if your player's character dies, it's time to subtract one from the number of lives available.

Using ++ and -- makes this simpler. Using ++ is called an increment and using -- is called a decrement.

If we have any numeric variable and we want to add one to it, we can write it like this:

```
crystalsCollected++;
```

To subtract one, we would write:

```
livesRemaining--;
```

Note that this syntax does not assign a value to the variable. It changed the variable's value in place. There are a few advantages to using this format to quickly add or subtract one from a variable. First, it's faster and easier to type. It's also visually distinct, so that if another programmer looks at your code your intentions are clear. Lastly, since it only serves one purpose, it's harder to unintentionally change when you—or someone else—is editing that code in the future.

> Using `variableName++;` is the same as `variableName = variableName + 1;`. But using an increment or decrement has a few advantages over this format.

Conditionals

On to the next construct: conditionals. We know that each line of code is a command. We know that the instructions are executed one at a time, from top to bottom. Now what if there is a situation where we don't always want an instruction to be executed? Or what if we only want to trigger an instruction when certain conditions are met?

This is where conditionals come in. They tell the program to execute an instruction (or set of instructions) only if certain conditions are true.

The most basic and common conditional is an `if` statement. Translated into English, it might read: *If this condition is true, then do this.* `If` statements are written using the word if in the code. They are followed by a condition inside parentheses. Each if statement is only evaluated when the program arrives at the first line of the if statement.

An if statement is formatted like this:

```
if(thisConditionIsTrue)
{
        //Everything in the curly braces is the body.
        //if the condition is true..
        //the code in the body will run.
}
```

The part of the if statement inside the parentheses is called a condition. You'll remember that the part that is inside the curly braces is called the body. The program will only run the code in the body if the if statement condition evaluates as true. We can build up the complexity of our conditional statements with a number of different operators. We can combine smaller statements and compare each one to see whether they are true or not. It's important to remember that the entire condition must evaluate as true for the actions in the body to be evaluated. If the condition evaluates as false, all of the body of our if statement is skipped.

Let's look at some basic examples of conditions.

```
if (health<90)
```

We can see that we have a variable named health. If the value contained in health is less than 90, then the condition would be true. Let's look at another example:

```
if (currentSpeed>=maximumSpeed)
```

Here we are using a conditional to compare two variables. We might not know the values of those variables, but we don't need to. The program knows the values and whenever it encounters this if statement, it will compare those values and determine whether the variable currentSpeed is greater than or equal to the variable named maximumSpeed. If it is, anything in a following body would run. If not, the entire body would be skipped.

Related to the if statement is the if-else statement. This adds an "else" body which will run when the if statement portion evaluates as false.

FIGURE 1.4   if (artistHasCoffee) {//then artist is happy!}.

Logical Operators

Now that we understand how conditional statements work, we can express more complex scenarios with them. What if we have multiple conditions we would like to consider at once? We could have one if statement and then nest a second if statement in the body of the conditional. That way we would only run the inner if statement when we know both of the conditions are true.

Or...

We can connect our conditions using logical operators.

An if statement using logical operators is similar to one without, it just gives us more flexibility in how we want to describe our condition.

Now we can take multiple expressions—each that would have needed

Logical operators in programming are the same ones we use in mathematics. If you're familiar with them, they all work the same. Sometimes the symbols look slightly different. If you've no idea what we're talking about yet, have no fear! That's what we're here for.

to be their own condition in an `if` statement—and combine them. This makes our code more readable, gives us the tools to build more complex conditions, and simplifies the process of testing multiple expressions to determine our conditions. Remember how we aspire to laziness? This will help with that. Let's take a look at an example:

> We're going to start using the word "expression" below. In this context, an expression can be a lot of things, including an `if` statement. To be technical about it, an expression is a series of elements that can be read by the computer. To be less technical, an expression is sort of like a sentence.

```
if((expression)logicalOperator(expression))
{
        //The body runs if the entire if statement is
        true
}
```

Keep in mind that our entire condition still needs to be either true or false, just like in the `if` statement with a single condition. We also need to figure out how all our expressions relate to one another, and to the overall condition.

Here are the three logical operators we'll be covering and their symbols:

And (&&)

```
if((A) && (B))
```

This means that both expression A and expression B must be true for the condition to evaluate as true. If either is false, the whole condition is false and any code in the body following would be skipped.

As an example, say we wanted to execute some code when we had at least 3 apples and less than 4 oranges. We could write that as:

```
if((apples >= 3)&&(oranges < 4))
{
}
```

Notice that we have two expressions that we could have used separately. But we can connect them with a logical operator: AND (&&). Because we used an AND, both expressions have to be true for the overall condition to be true.

Or (||)

```
if((A)||(B))
```

This means expression A or expression B can be true for the overall condition to be true. Only one needs to be true for the whole condition to be considered true.

If we wanted to execute some code when we had less than 7 apples or our truck is empty, we could write it as:

```
if((apples<7)||(truckEmpty))
{
}
```

Because we used an OR(||), only one of the conditions has to be met in order for the statement to evaluate as true.

Not (!)

```
if(!A)
```

This means the opposite of expression A. If A was false, it will now evaluate to true. If A was true, it will evaluate to false. This one is a little different from the other two, so we're going to take a closer look.

Say we have a variable called enemiesInSight that was set, at the moment, to false. That means there are no enemies in sight. Now, say we want a bit of music or dialog to run when there are no enemies in sight.

If we just stuck enemiesInSight in the condition of an if statement the code would only run when enemies were visible. So instead we use the NOT(!) operator to get the functionality we want by writing the following:

```
if (!enemiesInSight)
```

Now the code block that followed would only run when no enemies were in sight, because we are using the opposite of our variable.

Combos

Technically, we can combine as many expressions as we want. We can use AND(&&) multiple times like this:

```
if((A)&&(B)&&(C)&&(D))
```

Or OR(||) like this:

```
if((A)||(B)||(C)||(D))
```

In the first example, all of the expressions would need to be true for the overall condition to be true. In the second, only one needs to be true for the overall condition to be true.

Finally, we can mix and match and nest. If it gets hard to figure out which expression belongs to which logical operator, we can group them with more parentheses. Like so:

```
if ((A)&&(B)&&((C)||(D)))
```

You would read this example as: if A and B are true, and either C or D are true.

As you can see, this can get pretty complex. But the added flexibility saves space and can be used to write more detailed conditions.

Those three are the most common logical operators, and with that we have only one construct left to talk about in this chapter...

Loops

Up until now, we've been learning how to write code that executes and finishes. The script is read through and completed. One and done. But what if we want something to repeat? What if we would like a program to repeat as long as the player has not quit? What if we want an enemy patrol to repeat the same route after it has completed it once? This is where loops come in.

Loops are a tool used to repeat certain sections of code. Uses for loops are nearly unlimited and they are one of the most powerful tools in programming.

Do you remember when we talked about programmers being lazy? And making the computer do the work for us? Loops are one of the most useful ways to do that. If we wanted a program to generate the numbers 1 to 100 without loops, we'd need to write out a hundred lines of code. With loops, however, we can do this with one block of code. We can tell the program where to start and where to finish, and it will do the work for us.

We can also include the whole program in a loop, to ensure that it restarts after it is completed. Think of the way an ATM works. Once we've completed our transaction, an ATM starts over at the beginning—ready for the next customer to start a new transaction.

We could also use a loop to continuously check a score to see if the player has completed a level in a game. The list goes on and on.

All loops are made up of two parts: (1) the condition and (2) the body. Just like `if` statements. Again, the condition is the part that's evaluated as either true or false. If the condition is true, the body will run. The difference between a loop and an `if` statement being that after the body of the loop has executed, it will evaluate the condition again to see whether or not it should execute again. When the condition evaluates to false, the loop stops.

There are three types of loops. Let's talk about all of them!

Each time the body of a loop executes, it's called an iteration. If the loop runs three times, it has had three iterations.

while *loops*

`while` loops are the simplest, easiest to use and to understand. They repeat while a condition is true. `while` loops look like this:

```
while (condition)
{
      //body will run!
}
```

You may have noticed that this construct parallels the `if` statements we talked about. A `while` loop is essentially an `if` statement on repeat. Instead of evaluating the condition and executing the body once like an `if` statement, a `while` loop will continue to repeat while the condition remains true.

We can write a while loop like so:

```
while(livesLeft > 0)
{
      //give the player another chance
}

while(continuePlaying)
{
      //continue playing the game
}
```

Conditions can be as simple or as complex as the examples we explored for `if` statements. Remember, the whole condition must evaluate to true for the loop to run.

do while *loops*

The difference between a while loop and a do while loop is that a do while loop is always run at least once. They function exactly like while loops, but the first time the block is reached the program will run the body and then evaluate the condition. After that, it behaves like a normal while loop. When the condition is reached, it is evaluated to see if we need another iteration. Put simply, do while loops are upside down while loops. This is how we write a do while loop:

```
do
{
        //play the game
}while(continuePlaying);
```

So when would we want to use a do while loop instead of a while loop? When we want to make sure we run at least one iteration. Looking at our example above, to give the player one chance at playing the game before testing to see if the loop should run again, use a do while loop.

for *loops*

The previous two types of loops are great if we want to base our iterations on whether something is true or false. What if we'd like to count from one number to another? Or what if we'd like to increase a number until it is equal to a different number? This is where for loops come in.

A for loop runs for a certain number of iterations.

We write a for loop like this:

```
for(int i = startingNumber; condition; modifier)
{
        //body of the loop
}
```

On inspection, you'll see that the code inside the parentheses of the for loop is divided into three separate sections by semicolons.

The first variable tells the loop where to start. Since we use for loops to start counting, we need to pick a number to start from. This is a new variable, just for use within this for loop. We can actually name this variable whatever we like, but by convention it's called i. i stands for iterator, since we are using it to iterate through the loop or count.

The next section of our `for` loop is the condition. The condition works in the same way it did in the `while` loop and the `do while` loop. As long as the condition is true, the loop will continue with another iteration. The question the condition asks is some-

To iterate means to go through a process over and over. Each iteration brings us closer to our goal or end point for the `for` loop.

thing like this: Is `i` greater than, less than, etc... another number?

The last section is our modifier. We can use this to modify our variable `i`. If `i` never changes, our loop will never end. We need to modify our variable to keep our loop moving. You'll often find one of two things in the modifier section: `i++` or `i--`. If we're counting up by one until we reach our target, we can use `i++` to do so until we reach our goal. If we're counting down to a number by ones, we can use `i--` to subtract one from `i` for each iteration until we reach our target. There are other commands we can use to modify `i`, but those two are the most common by far.

Let's look at a few examples of `for` loops:

```
for(int i = 0; i < = 10; i++)
{
}
```

This loop will count from 0 to 10 for us. Note, we can use our variable `i` inside the body of the loop. We can add it to other variables. We can print out the value of `i` in our current iteration. We just want to be careful not to modify `i` itself while in the loop, because it's already being changed by the modifier in the modifier part of the `for` loop.

A loop that never ends is called an infinite loop. Infinite loops can be caused by any type of logic error that prevents the loop condition from evaluating as false. If you happen to cause an infinite loop, your program will either lock up, terminate, or let you know that there is an infinite loop and give you the option to terminate it.

```
for(int i = currentHealth; i > minimumHealth; i--)
{
}
```

In this example, we initialize `i` as the value of another variable called `currentHealth`. We're continuing to iterate this loop for as long as `i` is greater than `minimumHealth`. We can set and compare the value of `i` to any other variable. We don't need to know, or even keep track, of those values. We're making the computer do the work for us.

THOSE ARE THE BASICS

So, to recap: Programming languages each have a format and syntax, which must be followed for the computer to understand what we're trying to tell it. Variables are the information you've given to the computer, and operators are how you manipulate that information. Conditionals give us flexibility, and let us have more control over what code runs when. Logical operators allow us to create more complex conditions, and loops let us repeat code under certain conditions.

These are the simplest constructs in programming. We will get into more complicated ones a little later, but don't underestimate the power of some simple programming to make beautiful, creative, and fun games.

CHAPTER 2

Introduction to Game Engines

Y OU MADE IT THROUGH the Introduction to Programming! We covered the basics of computer programming. You're not going to need all the details we covered at your fingertips for this chapter. An understanding of the bigger concepts—programs execute in order, each line of code is usually one instruction, etc.—is good, but we're going to go in a different direction now: toward games!

Now we get to start breaking down games more specifically, rather than programming in general.

Games are things we play, things we design, things we are able to interact with, and all video games are run on computers. Whether a mobile game, a handheld or home console game, or a PC game—those are all run on types of computers. And what else does that tell us? If all games are run on computers, then all video games are programs. This is true from your oldest Game Boy title, to the newest *next-gen* game.

In this chapter, we're going to talk about game engines—their history, how they work, and what they do for us as game makers. We'll also look at a few game engines specifically and talk about how to choose your game engine. You'll also find a section discussing shaders—which are small programs that create visual effects—and another on physics engines—the part of your game engine that provides you with realistic (or not-so-realistic) physics.

GAME ENGINES

What is a game engine? A game engine runs your game and is a part of your game. *Engine* is a good way to think about it. We build the game around the engine—and the game is both the engine and your code working together.

There are lots of different game engines to choose from these days, and they've all got slightly different functionality. For most of the chapter, we'll be talking about the functionality that all game engines share, rather than looking at the details of specific engines. Now, we're sure you always wondered how game engines came to be.

A Brief History...

Once upon a time, in the early days of game development, games were the engines and the engines were the games. They were nearly inseparable. After a team shipped a game, they would start their next project from scratch. There would be places where they could borrow and reuse pieces of code, but essentially the team needed to assemble a new engine for this new game.

Later on came reusable game engines. Teams began to spend time upfront on writing a larger engine (an engine that might end up doing more than would be utilized in a single specific game). This way they wouldn't need to start from scratch for the next project. Not only that, but keeping the same engine for more than one game meant that reusing code across projects became much easier.

And finally, teams and companies realized that the engines they built in-house could be useful to teams outside their company. If an outside team didn't have the resources to create an engine from the ground up themselves, they might be able to pay the licensing fees to use someone else's game engine. Then the outside team would be able to customize and adapt it to their needs. This is largely the model that is in existence today. Though there are now also companies that write game engines, with the intention of selling or licensing them directly to studios and game developers, and don't make games at all.

Under the Hood

Game engines can be written in a wide variety of programming languages. And you'll often see more than one programming language

In-house refers to technology that is created by a company and is specifically for use within that company.

being used in one game engine—though you'll likely only be using one yourself. Which languages are used are dependent on the target platforms and sometimes game engines have their own variants of a programming language used for scripting.

> Target platform refers to the system, device, or type of computer where your game will eventually be run. This could be a mobile phone, a handheld console, or a computer running Linux.

Traditionally, the core of a game engine is written in a robust general-purpose programming language such as C++ or C#. This is done because compiled languages (remember: compiled programming languages are read all the way through and then run; interpreted programming lan-

> Scripting is just a fancy term for writing code. It's generally used for writing your code in game engines, rather than writing the code for a game engine.

guages are read and run line-by-line) execute faster and thus help the game to run faster once it's finished.

The downside to using the compiled languages is that any changes to the code—large or small—require the whole engine to be recompiled. With some engines, this could take many hours.

Scripting inside the engine, on the other hand, favors the more lightweight interpreted languages. Interpreted scripts are only read by the program when it was executed. Changes can be quickly made without having to recompile anything; sometimes changes can even be made while the game is running. This allows for the game designers to quickly test, refine, and iterate on their designs without recompiling anything.

Today, engines are often written and scripted in the same language. There are a few reasons for this trend. It reduces complexity. When you have multiple languages tied together in a single game, it can get quite complex. Using the same language for the core engine and the scripting also allows the game designers and core engine programmers to speak the same *language*. This can reduce the mental load on the team by simplifying communication. Also, a number of technologies have advanced and the build times aren't as long anymore.

Even interpreted languages run fast enough for a game now. So you'll get engines written in JavaScript (an interpreted language) and games scripted in JavaScript in that engine too.

GAME LOOPS

Recall that at its most basic, a program is a series of instructions to be followed in order. Remember our dance chart from Chapter 1? Or the sheet music?

So, the series of commands are what we write when we write code. Now that we're *under the hood* of the game engine, let's take a look at what that engine is doing with those commands and how they are processed. This will get technical. It's useful to know as you start to build off of your game engine, even if it may not seem like it relates directly to your projects.

All games share something called a game loop. We've talked about different kinds of loops in Chapter 1. A game loop is a special type of loop responsible for updating the state of your game and moving it forward, so to speak. The game loop will continue to loop as long as the game is running and is part of the reason games are programs that respond to input and operate in real time.

Two steps happen in our game loop: (1) an update step and (2) a render step (Figure 2.1). A completed set of update and render steps are one iteration of the game loop. Each iteration produces one frame.

The Basics: Update and Render Phases

Update and render are both programming commands. They in turn run other commands. We're going to go through how they work and their purposes in detail. In order to get a first, rough idea of how they work, think of a dramatic play.

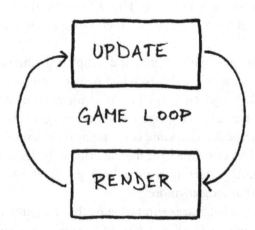

FIGURE 2.1   A game loop.

Imagine a stage, with a large curtain and a number of actors onstage.

Now imagine that the actors are not allowed to move when anyone is looking at them. They can only move when the curtain is down. When the curtain drops, they're allowed to move. Finally, imagine that each actor has a set of instructions that they will follow in order—one each time the curtain falls. So, the curtain falls, they follow an instruction and the curtain rises.

Now, imagine the curtain rising and falling faster. Like, really fast.

> You will sometimes see a third step in a game loop: Get Input. This refers to the interactive nature of games and divides receiving the player's input (through a keyboard, mouse controller, or other interaction) into a separate step. We're including that as part of our update step. It will depend on whom you are talking to.

You'd get the illusion that they are moving, yes? Even if they never actually moved when you could see them. When you get to imagining that curtain falling and rising many times per second, you're getting into how games work.

When the curtain is down and the actors are following their instructions, that's our update phase. When the curtain is up and we can see the result of the actors following their instructions, that's the render phase (Figure 2.2). Most video games aim to drop and raise the curtain either 30 times a second or 60 times a second. For virtual reality games, the rate goes up to at least 90 times per second. This rate at which the screen updates is called the frames per second (FPS).

> 30 FPS to 60 FPS has been the standard since early video games. Even early some games were running at 60 FPS.

Delta Time

In our play analogy, delta time (DT) is the amount of time the curtain is down measured in milliseconds—hiding the update phase from the audience. It's the time between one frame and the next. This becomes useful as you create objects that have to do things like move across a screen—you're going to want to know how far you want the object to move between one frame and the next. The reason we have delta time to track that is because frame rates vary and so does the processing power of different computers—we can't count on the amount of time between one frame and another being perfectly even. So, delta time tracks that.

FIGURE 2.2 Do you think the ladybugs can pull off 30FPS?

There are other reasons to understand delta time, but even this simple one will help you think more like a programmer when you are working on your games.

The Details: Running Speed

In Chapter One, we looked at some basic programs. Games obviously get much more complicated than those simple programs, but the basic principles still apply. Our code executes one line at a time and can store values, retrieve values, modify values, and print or report values to the user. We can also group bits of code together in things called methods and classes (which you can explore in the "Introduction to Object-Oriented Programming" chapter).

So, even though a game may have thousands, hundreds of thousands, or even millions of lines of code, they all follow the same principles. And a game engine reads a simple program the same way it reads a complex one.

Most game engines are designed to run with their update phase at a fixed rate with a delay. This means that the speed at which the program is run is determined by the engine—not by how quickly the computer could run it. This fixed rate allows the game to run the same speed on a slow computer and a fast computer. Among other things, this keeps it fair if two people are playing the same game against one another on their own computers. A powerful computer doesn't run the game faster.

A faster computer can run the frame rate faster. That doesn't increase the speed at which the update step is processed and produced on screen.

Here's how it works: On each computer, after the update and render steps complete, the game engine checks to see if it has time to spare. If there's time to spare, the computer waits until it's time to start the next update step.

The Details: Engine Code

When it comes to the code of your game, it can be divided into two parts: engine code and game code (Figure 2.3). Engine code is the code that makes up the game engine—and it's unlikely that you will be able to or would want to mess with that. Game code is the code you write in the engine. When you open a game engine (like Unity or Unreal), you'll have an interface that lets you write your own game code into it. When you do that, you're building onto and around the engine code that's already there. Though you won't be seeing the engine code, a holistic understanding of what it does will help you as you are making your games.

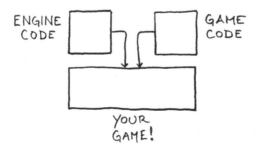

FIGURE 2.3   engineCode + gameCode == game!

With that in mind, engine code is the core of the game engine: this code takes care of rendering and showing the objects on screen, gives us the functionality to play audio and animations, or even ensures that your game runs on multiple platforms. The engine code is always written by the makers of the engine, and the idea is that the functionality of the game engine can be relied upon. Often the engine code will be proprietary code and will be unavailable for us to modify or even see. We use game engines so that we don't have to work out things like creating the code that will perform an update or render step.

Game engines are written to allow game developers to insert parts of their own code; this is how we're able to utilize all of the functionality built into the game engine. We're able to build off the foundation of the engine code. We can choose what parts we want to use, refine how things work in our game worlds, and add our own code on top of the game engine, all without rewriting anything in the engine itself.

The Details: Update Phase

So, the update phase is the *when the curtain is down* part in our play analogy. It's the first part of the game loop (which repeats at least 30 times every second, leading to the illusion of motion and to our game *running*). The update phase is designed to tell each piece of code, that it's time to perform the next action.

Even though update is in some ways one step, it might include hundreds of different methods and processes that need to run in order to update what's happening in the game. The update phase is designed to tell each object, each bit of code, to figure out the next action that it needs to perform. It may tell the physics system that it's time to calculate the next step for an object in motion, it may tell the web chat functionality to check to see if there are any new messages. It will also do things like checking to see what buttons the player has recently or is currently pressing, so that it can ready the appropriate response to that input.

It's important to keep in mind that computers don't perform actions instantly, even if it is very fast.

Time for a new analogy! Let's imagine a game that has a wolf in it. If our wolf character needs to walk from point A to point B, it doesn't just happen. First, the wolf character needs to have something happen to determine why it will move to point B. Let's say it caught the delicious scent of the player character. The scent detection code will be in the wolf's code, but the wolf is told by the update method to run all the sections of code that need updating.

So, in one update step, we'll trigger the code that simulates our wolf character catching the scent of the player character. Once the wolf catches the players scent, a calculation will need to happen to figure out where the wolf needs to go. This might be calculated in the next update step—if it's simple—or in multiple steps—if it's complicated. Once the target location is determined, the wolf character is on it's way! Since things happen in steps in game code, we need to gradually move the wolf character to their destination—the delicious player. If we simply told the wolf to move there once we found the target location, it would vanish and then appear at the target location. Which would be sad for our player.

So each time the update method is called, it will tell the wolf to update all the sections of code that need updating. Since we already have a scent, we just need to tell the wolf to move toward the target at point B. How fast should the wolf move though? At some point the designer would have chosen a good speed for a wolf and might have stored it in a variable called `int wolfSpeed = 13.50` (this number represents meters per second within the game world).

Now we might assume we can just tell the wolf: when you have a scent, head to the target direction at `wolfSpeed`. Not quite. If we used `wolfSpeed` at this point, it would move 13.50 meters each step! In other words, after one second the wolf would have moved 405 meters or about a quarter of a mile! A quarter of a mile in one second might be a bit too fast for a wolf.

So, this is how we get the wolf to move at a reasonable rate: We can divide the wolf's speed by 30 (our target frame rate). Now we end up with `int wolfSpeed = 0.45`, and with each step the wolf moves forward 0.45 meters. Awesome! Now our wolf speeds along at 0.45 meters each step, or 13.50 meters per second, which is about 30 miles per hour.

Now, we have one more thing to look at before we're set.

Right now, we have a system where each time our update step runs, we move our wolf 0.45 meters; our movement speed is tied to our update speed. Think about our game running on slow computers. If it lag and starts running at 15 FPS, then what happens? That means that in one second our wolf only ran 6.75 meters, half as much as we wanted. In extremely slow situations, games may even skip entire frames to catch up. This would mess up our calculations even more.

This is where delta time comes in. Recall that delta time is the time since the last frame was completed. The way this is designed is to let us choose the speed we want over the course of one second. So to fix this we want to change our movement speed back to `int wolfSpeed = 13.50`. Then when it's time to move the wolf, we can do the following: `wolfSpeed` `*deltaTime`. This ensures that the wolf's speed is divided appropriately.

To talk about delta time, let's move from our wolf character briefly to a cake. Yes, a cake. Imagine one second as a cake. Our entire cake represents the whole second. Optimally, for a game running at 30 FPS, we want 30 frames in our second—that means 30 equal slices of our cake.

Unfortunately, FPS varies. Lots of actions can cause things to slow down, and sometimes this can cause lag. So instead of trying to depend on a consistent frame rate when we use `wolfSpeed` `*deltaTime`, the delta time part takes care of *slicing* our `wolfSpeed` to the appropriate size. Which in this case is 13.50.

Let's look at an extreme case. If our game was running at 2 FPS, delta time would become 0.5. Meaning, it was half a second since the last frame was completed. If we're multiplying `wolfSpeed` by 0.5 we'll get 6.75. This means our two frames add up to 13.50. If we were running at 8 FPS we'd get back 1.6875. So our 8 frames will still add 13.50 over one second. Obviously, we don't want our game running on single-digit FPS, but if it was, then delta time would help our wolf's speed stay consistent. No matter how our frame rate varies, if we're multiplying a value by delta time it'll mean that our initial value of 13.50 will be sliced up perfectly each frame, so that over a second it still equals 13.50; no matter what the FPS, our wolf will move at 13.50.

What if the game ran on a super powerful computer at 200 FPS? Does the wolf run at 90 meters per second? Not quite. After the update and render steps, our game engines check to see if it's time for them to run the next update phase. If it's too early, it'll wait until it's time to run again. This is the mechanism that prevents games from running too fast on more powerful systems.

We just explored one example in detail—one wolf in our imaginary game. Now imagine a pack of wolves and perhaps a few bears in this game. All of these are being updated every frame. That's a lot of code being run multiple times every second.

In certain situations, something will change so much in our game world that the computer isn't going to be able to update everything in our game in a single frame. When this happens, the game engine can be made to spread out the calculations across multiple frames and perhaps multiple seconds in order to avoid lag. But this is for situations like—if the player does something that fills the entire environment with trees and parrots. That may be a bit too much to do in one frame.

That's a look at what's going on in our game engine during the update phase. Note that there may be variations on the update step that run too. Specialized versions of the update step might be used for the physics engine, to check up on the characters, or on other systems. This is still all done by the engine without our having to explicitly program it.

So, when the update phase is over and the engine has read the code and logic and knows what's coming next, we need to move on to the render phase and actually get it in front of our players. Let's spend some time exploring how we get pictures and the visual aspects of games to appear on the screen.

The Details: Render Phase

Now we know each frame has an update step, followed by a render step. Next, we're looking at what exactly is happening in this render step. The *video* part of video games means that we're able to interact with a moving picture on a screen. We've talked about the code behind the games, how that's divided up, and how the update phase sets it in motion. Rendering is the process of generating images from that code and getting it to the screen.

On Graphics Hardware

We're headed toward the rendering pipeline, but first we're going to talk about the hardware that makes that pipeline possible. The process of taking the information in game and producing an image on a screen is called rendering. In today's games all rendering happens on graphics hardware: a Graphics Processing Unit (GPU).

The purpose of a Graphics Processing Unit (GPU) is similar to a Central Processing Unit (CPU), but they approach running programs in different ways. A CPU is designed to be versatile. A CPU is able to tackle many different programs, written in any number of languages, and describing old or new programs. CPUs can also run a few processes in parallel. Unlike a CPU, GPUs are designed to run a specific type of program (shaders) and they can run a lot of processes in parallel.

A video card contains a GPU, but the GPU is the part of the video card that does all of the actual rendering work. There are two types of GPUs: dedicated (also referred to as a discrete GPU) and integrated. An integrated GPU means they are built into a CPU, whereas a dedicated GPU is separate.

Dedicated GPUs are separate chips in a device designed for rendering or in completely separate cards that can be added into PCs. These function the same way an integrated GPU does, except they are many times more powerful. This allows for more detailed graphics, faster frame rates, and more advanced effects. Integrated GPUs are cheaper to manufacture and less powerful, and they also consume less energy (important for devices that run on battery). Integrated GPUs are common in low power devices such as mobile phones, handheld consoles, and low powered laptops. One downside to integrated GPUs is that they are not upgradeable—whereas you can upgrade a dedicated GPU card.

> *Dedicated* and *integrated* when they are used to describe a GPU is referring to whether the GPU has its own memory or not. A dedicated GPU has its own memory. An integrated GPU is using the memory of the machine it's attached to.

In graphics programming, we are technically able to access the functions of the GPU directly if we really wanted to. But this is more advanced work than we're going to cover. Instead, we use Graphics API tools to help standardize the GPU commands that we can use. Today the two most popular graphics APIs are OpenGL and DirectX. Modern video cards support both APIs. Occasionally specific functionality is only designed to work on a specific manufacturer's video cards, but that's not something to worry about at this point.

> API stands for Application Programming Interface. APIs are pieces of code that can serve as a connection between the engine code and an outside application or library. If, for instance, we wanted to use Google Maps in our game, we'd need to use the Google Maps API to make that connection.

Since we're not writing game engines, we don't even need to worry much about the graphics APIs. They are working to render things behind the scenes in the GPU. Your game engine will have a list of features that includes whether it supports OpenGL, DirectX, or both; most game engines today support both.

The last thing to note about GPUs is that they are specifically designed to do lots and lots of simple tasks very fast. GPUs are specialized hardware; it's not easy to get them to do anything except rendering. But... if you give a GPU a specific set of instructions, it will have them complete very quickly. Part of this is how they are designed and the other part is that it's able to run thousands of instructions in parallel. So rather than giving one instruction, waiting for it to complete, then giving it the next instruction, we can give it thousands of instructions to complete at once and it will work to finish them all simultaneously.

And why is this useful information to have in the back of your heads, you ask?

Because the GPU is what runs shaders. And shaders are cool.

Objects in 3D Games

If you have a background in 3D modeling, you'll be familiar with this, but for those who do not...

In a 3D game, each of our objects is made up of 3D models or meshes. All of these meshes are collectively referred to as geometry. A mesh is a series of triangles or quads arranged and textured to resemble an object. Think about it as a really detailed 3D paper model: there is nothing on the inside, but when you cut, tape, glue, and fold the shapes together, they create an object. Each one of the triangles and/or quads is represented as a series of points: A triangle has three points and a quad has four. In games and graphics programming, each of these points is called a vertex.

> A *quad* refers to a quadrilateral face on a model—any two-dimensional shape that's made up of four points and four straight lines.

Once you have your model, the texture on the individual faces creates the detail. You can think of textures as the wallpapering we wrap around the mesh. We can have multiple types of textures each responsible for a different effect. Different textures may be responsible for color, shininess and bumpiness. Others may be responsible for giving the effect of additional detail to the model.

Shaders

This is a topic that is worth an entire book, but we want to demystify shaders and help you to understand what they are and how they work if this is your introduction to them.

A shader is a piece of code used to create a visual effect in a program. You see the results of shaders anytime you see anything in a modern game. Some shaders are simple and only responsible for rendering a 2D character on screen. Shaders can also be very complex and take into account the color of the material, the angle of lights, and even properties of the object itself—such as health or experience level—before determining what something looks like on screen.

Other types of shaders can be used to move, resize, and change the geometry of certain objects on the fly—rather than having to produce those results in a modeling program. When you see an ocean or a lake or a puddle with ripples in a game, the waves themselves will probably be the results of shaders. The actual model may be a plane—a flat rectangle—but a shader is used to produce waves and have them ripple across the surface; no modeling or animation was needed to create that effect. A related technique is often used to animate grass, bushes, or trees swaying in the wind. Remember our wolf from the update section? We could use a shader to give motion to her fur. Rather than taking the time to model and animate those motions, we can do that work by writing a shader.

Shaders can get fairly complicated if you want, but they aren't scary. To use them effectively, it's a good idea to have a solid understanding of what's going on in the render phase—which is what we're getting to, we promise. We're going to talk about what shaders do here and how they work, and then we'll delve into the rendering pipeline.

At their most basic level, shaders are just simple programs. That's it! No magic, no chaos, no wizardry. If we think about the programs described in chapter one, shaders are not much different. The two primary differences between those programs and shaders are (1) they run on the GPU and not the CPU, which means that (2) shaders have very narrow purposes.

GPUs, as part of the rendering pipeline, run our shaders. GPUs use highly specialized hardware along with shaders to run hundreds or even thousands of computations at the same time. Since shaders are simple programs, they are well suited to be divided up and run simultaneously. Since a GPU needs to process all the data to create a single frame, it's performing a large number of those calculations at the same time (Figure 2.4).

Types of Shaders   The two main types of shaders are vertex shaders and fragment shaders. They each perform different functions, but their purposes are similar. They take input data in one format, run the shader, and send the output down the graphics pipeline.

Vertex shaders are designed to work on vertices as their input data; the result when they are finished are called primitives. Primitives are the simple shapes made by connecting vertices—and we'll talk more about them in the upcoming section on the rendering pipeline. Fragment shaders

FIGURE 2.4   Shaders can create all sorts of different visual effects!

receive fragments (which are potential pixels) as their input and output the finished pixels as their result.

Other newer types of shaders are geometry shaders (used to add additional geometry to a scene), tessellation shader (used to add additional detail to meshes), and compute shaders for GPGPU purposes.

General-Purpose Computing on Graphics Processing Units (GPGPU) is a newer technique that uses the power of GPUs to run programs or calculations that would usually be run on a CPU. This can free up the CPU to do other things. It's not suited for every problem but is a great new tool. It can also be used to solve problems in a hybrid manner in ways not previously possible. GPGPU has been used to dynamically place vegetation in game, perform calculations to make AI more efficient, and even outside of games to perform scientific calculations.

Rendering Pipeline

It's time! We're going to talk about the rendering pipeline (Figure 2.5)—which makes up the Render phase of our game loop and produces the image players will see on their screens.

If you'll recall, in a game our scenes consist of a number of meshes that make up our geometry. How does that eventually produce the graphics that we see when we're playing?

You can think of the rendering pipeline as an assembly line. It's a series of separate steps, each with a purpose. All the steps work together to finish a complete picture. But, this is only one picture. Remember that games target either 30 FPS or 60 FPS? So everything in our pipeline needs to happen continually, at the rate of at least 30 FPS. The computing speed necessary to accomplish this is why we have dedicated hardware in the form of GPUs.

So, let's walk through the different steps in the graphics pipeline, look at what they do, and how they work together to produce the final image.

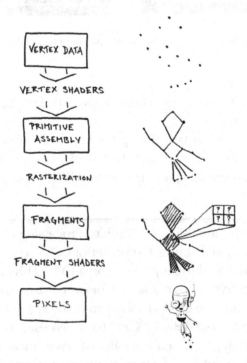

FIGURE 2.5 The basics of the rendering pipeline.

Our scenes are made up of geometry. The first step in rendering is breaking down all of our geometry into their vertex data. This vertex data is then fed into the GPU and becomes the first part of the rendering pipeline.

This is where we encounter our first shader. Right now, all we have to work with is vertex data, so the shaders at this point in the pipeline are vertex shaders. Vertex shaders allow us to perform calculations and make adjustments to on the vertices. And if you'll recall, vertex shaders produce data called primitives—the simple shapes that will make up the faces of our models.

The next step in the pipeline is primitive assembly. Once we determine where all of our vertices have ended up—especially if we moved or edited them since the last frame with a vertex shader—we need to connect them to start constructing the geometry. With primitive assembly, the GPU starts connecting the vertices to create triangles and quads, and continues the process of building our image.

The next step is clipping. In order to figure out what we need to render on the screen, we need to figure out what the player is looking at and what they should see. In a game engine, this is done with a camera. The camera information was fed into the GPU along with all the other data. Before we perform any further calculations, we want to make sure we're not trying to render anything behind the camera. If the player isn't looking at something, it's pointless to render it. We only want to render what the camera is pointing at.

So, we clip what behind the first part of our camera, cropping everything the camera can't see. This is called the near or front clipping plane. We can also clip things that are too far from the camera, to help cut down on the number of objects we need to render. This is called the far or back clipping plane. All geometry that is clipped at this point is discarded by the GPU and will not be rendered. If you're thinking this was wasteful, just remember: GPUs are extremely efficient when it comes to simultaneous calculations.

> The camera we're referring to is a piece of functionality that your game engine will provide and that you'll be able to set up in your game.

In the next step, the GPU creates a viewing frustum (Figure 2.6). A frustum is a pyramid like shape starting small near the camera and extending out to encompass everything the camera sees. Anything that falls outside of our view frustum is cut from rendering as well.

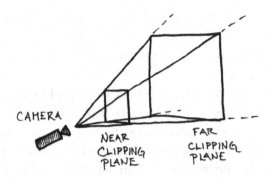

FIGURE 2.6 Whatever is inside our view frustum will be rendered.

So, up until this point the GPU has: taken a stream of vertices, run a vertex shader to translate or adjust them if applicable, assembled primitive shapes from our vertices, and clipped our geometry, so we're only rendering what the player will actually see.

With all that done, we still only have vertices and geometry—not a complete image representing our game. In order to complete our final frame, we need a few more steps.

Our next step is rasterization. A raster image is a series of pixels in a grid and rasterization is where we take all of the data the GPU has constructed so far and start to move toward producing pixels on a screen.

To visualize the way rasterization works, imagine every pixel on our screen as a square in a grid. Next, align that grid with our view frustum. Now we can look through any hole in that grid and project a straight line until it collides with a piece of geometry. The GPU is able to figure out what we hit with that line and what sort of pixel should be rendered there. But we're not quite at rendering pixels yet. When our line hits a piece of geometry, rather than creating a pixel we end up with something called a fragment. Remember that a fragment is a potential pixel. All of the fragments will run through a fragment shader—even if all that shader does is turning the fragment into a pixel. Fragment shaders can do a lot of other things—they allow for more changes to happen before finally producing our pixel. We're going to spend a bit of time on this step and how a fragment shader works below.

A pixel is a square of color on a large grid—and when we put enough of them together and look at them from far enough away they form an image on a screen. One difference between a fragment and a pixel is that a fragment still exists in 3D space, whereas a pixel is a square in our image. You can almost think of fragments as 3D pixels. Fragments are already aligned within our grid, the grid that will eventually become the grid for our pixels. Their position is set.

Fragments contain a lot of information: they can have a color, a depth, texture coordinates, and other values. All of this information is processed in a shader to help change a fragment into a pixel. Some of this information will determine what color our final pixel will be—it will depend on what fragment shaders we use.

A fragment shader will perform texture mapping. The shader looks at

At this point, because the fragments are already aligned with the grid the same way our pixels will be, vertices and vertex shaders have already finished their work when we reach this step.

A texture in this context is a pattern of colors that lends more detail to an object in our game.

the texture on the object our fragment falls on. When we find out which part of the texture aligns with our fragment we have a texture sample or a color to work from. There are many different types of texture sampling. Each of them is a trade-off between memory use and detail.

Then, depending on what sort of effects are going to be at work in the scene the shaders finally produce, they may do a variety of things from here. They might take into account the lighting in the scene or other visual information. When all the applicable shaders have run, the information will come together to determine a final color value—and that will be the pixel.

Now that we understand a bit of how fragment shaders work, what can we do with them? Here's an example: a variable representing time in our game might be combined with a texture—so that the texture shifts over time in our game. If the texture looked like energy waves and was transparent, we could use this effect on our model to look like an energy shield. Rather than being a static effect, it could move over the surface of the object. We can adjust those colors too. Using the fragment shader we can tint the textures as well, adjusting the color dynamically in the game.

This is just one example on how we could adjust the way things look in our game with a fragment shader. There's a lot of information in our fragments that we can manipulate to produce different visual effects.

The output of the fragment shader or shaders is finally pixels! Hooray!

So, do we just write them out to the screen and call it a day? Not quite. If the results went directly to the screen, it would have some undesired side effects. We might not get consistent results. Some parts might not update at the same time and we don't have as much control. Rather than writing to the screen, we instead write to something called a buffer. A buffer is like a staging area for all of our brand new beautiful pixels. As we're

A buffer stores visual information temporarily before it's shown on the screen. After we have a grid of fragments, we're at another shader step! This time we're able to use fragment shaders.

writing to the buffer, the last frame written to the buffer is being displayed. Once the time is up for the image currently being displayed, the buffer is displayed onscreen all at once. Meanwhile, we're able to write the next incoming frame to the buffer.

And that's it! There ends our rendering pipeline. When combined with our update phase it makes a single step in our game loop. It's a lot to do at least 30 times a second, yes?

Optimized Images

Sometimes, when we have a lot to render it will take longer than intended and we might run out of time before we've had chance to complete the new buffer. In this case, the buffer goes out as an incomplete image. This is called a torn frame and you might notice it as an odd line somewhere in the screen, usually seen in a highly detailed area or ones with a lot of action.

Vertical sync or v-sync can help avoid this by writing the buffer out to the screen when the screen itself refreshes. This means the game will only render as fast as the screen is designed to refresh.

Another technique to help avoid torn frames is a double (or even triple) buffer. This means instead of having one buffer before we write to the screen we have two or three. This means if we miss rendering something because we don't have enough time, we have one additional frame in the queue. If we need to catch up, we'll drop one of the frames in the queue to end up back where we should be. The nice thing with dropping a single frame is that it's usually not noticeable by the user.

PLACING OBJECTS IN A GAME

First things first: today both 2D and 3D game engines function nearly identically under the hood. The results may appear vastly different, but the technologies and techniques are largely the same. Some 2D game engines are actually 3D game engines where you can't move in and out along that third dimension.

When editing our game scenes (or levels) we're able to arrange objects, elements, and features. We're able to add characters, collectable items, scenery, and even invisible objects (such as triggers for cut scenes and events). All of these need a location.

In a game engine, objects are given a position on a 2D or 3D grid system, not unlike in a city's layout. In a city that's built on a grid, we have streets running north/south and streets running east/west. We can define a location on a 2D grid by choosing an intersection nearest the object we are placing. If we are working in a 3D space, think about adding the third dimension by adding the floor number of a building. In game engines, when we refer to an object's position we call it the transform.

In a 3D game engine, we keep track of the transform with respect to 3 axes (an axis or dimension is the same thing. But we use the terms axis and axes in game development). We use the x-axis (the east/west street in our city analogy), the y-axis (the floor number in our city analogy), and the z-axis (the north/south street in our city analogy) (See Figure 2.7).

We need to track where each object is on both axes (in 2D) or on all three axes (in 3D). We could do this with a separate variable for each axis. But—often we need to do calculations on two or three of the axes at once. So, it would be convenient to store them all together.

Enter vectors! On top of sounding really cool vectors are a data type that allow us to store multiple coordinates all together. The two most common types of vectors are `vector2` and `vector3`. The numbers that are being tracked in these data types are float values. If we used integers instead of floats we wouldn't be able to smoothly move objects from one place to another; our objects would appear to jerk or snap to the new positions as the integers are changed.

There is more than one sort of numerical data type we can store in a variable. We've talked about integers (`int`) in chapter one as a way to store whole numbers (no decimals or fractions). We're about to talk about floats. A `float` is a data type that holds a number with decimals in a variable. We'll talk about more data types in the Introduction to C#.

A `vector2` is used to track two axes: the x-axis and the y-axis. This is used for 2D games and for interaction in a 2D space.

```
Vector2 playerPosition = new Vector2(1.0f, 0.0f);
```

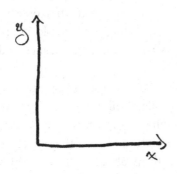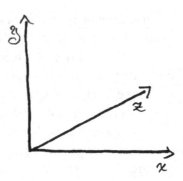

FIGURE 2.7 Representing our 3D axes.

A vector3 is used to track three axes: the x-axis, the y-axis, and z-axis. This is used for 3D games and interaction in 3D space. It could look like this (Figure 2.7):

```
Vector3 playerPosition = new Vector3(1.0f, 0.0f, 5.0f);
```

These are used to track the transform of something in your game. Vectors, though, are used to track a lot more than just a transform. For example, along with the location of our objects in game, they can also be used to track the rotation of our object. When we use the x, y, and z axes (a Vector3) to describe rotation it's called an Euler Angle.

PHYSICS

Now that we have an idea of how to define the location of an object in our game scene, it's time to talk about how that object behaves once it is there.

Physics are a normal part of games today. We expect our characters to move around and interact with different objects in the game. Maybe our heroine bumps into a stack of crates and knocks them over. Maybe she's chasing thieves and she hits one with a tranquilizer dart—we expect the thief to immediately fall asleep and their body to comically collapse.

Or maybe we are making a pinball simulator. The flippers fling the pinball around the play field. The ball should ricochet off bumpers, travel up and down ramps, and bounce off the walls.

When we use a game engine, we won't have to specifically program all those interactions.

Game engines come with a physics engine and while these do a couple of things for us, first and foremost, they simulate physics.

FIGURE 2.8 A few commonly used physics shapes.

Before the physics engine can get to work, we need to give it something to work on. This will not be the detailed model. The visual model would be far too complicated to calculate all the physics for—so often, we use a simpler invisible shape. The physics engine will give us a number of different simple shapes (Figure 2.8) that we can use in the physics engine— and we'll put our 2D or 3D art over them.

These simple shapes save in processing power. They each have a number of attributes that the physics engine uses when it's performing its calculations. The attributes can be things like: density, mass, friction, drag, angular drag, and more.

Physics engines also give us the ability to connect different shapes using joints and constraints. Different kinds of joints let us simulate things like: hinges, wheels on an axle, a hard connection, or even a spring connecting them. Constraints allow us to further define these joints—they might limit the rotation of a joint or the distance the two shapes can move from one another.

Once we have our physics shapes set up we don't need to move them at all, and it's better if we don't try to move the objects directly. We want to let the physics engine do the work. So we apply forces to the object instead.

Often in game engines, we might cause actual errors if we move something directly, rather than simulating its movement by applying forces to it. When we move an object directly, it looks to the physics engine as though we're causing an object to vanish and reappear. That can cause a number of unexpected results.

When we want a cube to move forward, we can apply a force to the cube. We can pick a large or small force, and then the physics engine will take into account the mass of the cube, the magnitude of the force, and the friction of the surface it's resting on (if applicable). Then the engine will simulate the results. In a simple racing game, we may simulate a force pushing the car to get it to move, and then let the wheels do the steering and rolling. In an advanced physics racing game, we'd simulate a force causing the wheels to rotate, which would calculate the friction with the ground along with the weight of the car and make the car move. The important thing is we didn't need to program any of the movement functionality by hand; we just need to set everything up and tell the physics engine to simulate. It will do the rest.

Most of the time when we're talking about physics, we're talking about something called rigidbody physics, which is differentiated from softbody physics. In rigidbody physics the physics shapes—or colliders—don't change. They never squish, stretch, dent, or deform. They always retain their original shape. Softbody physics, on the other hand, do change.

Physics interactions are generally pretty expensive—meaning they require a lot of processing effort—to simulate, so a number of tricks are employed to help keep the number of calculations reasonable. The more faces on a physics shape the more complex it is to calculate the physics interactions—remember what we said about the shape not being the same as a model?

Rather than having a detailed character with each limb accurately recreated and simulated in the physics engine, we might just use a capsule for two reasons. First: having a simpler physics model is much easier to calculate with. If we had a physics mesh—also called a collider—that matched our model it could make our game very slow, even nonfunctional. Second: using a capsule gets us the results we want without the overhead of an extremely detailed physics mesh.

If we are using a capsule for a human character, we want it sized a bit smaller than the model. This will prevent our character from walking through walls, it stops us when we bump into something appropriately, and it lets objects hit us. Using a capsule also has another small advantage: physics engines calculate physics mathematically, but they are only tuned to be precise up to a certain point. After that point, the physics are rounded off. We aren't going to notice if the capsule is off by a few centimeters. Cutting down on the precision helps make things run faster. Keep in mind, this rounding can produce slightly different results. If we have an online game that depends on physics, two different players may see different outcomes. Physics engines where we will always get ever so slightly varied results are called nondeterministic physics engines.

Choosing the right shapes for our objects can make a big difference too. We can't account for every small specific detail that might effect a real-life physics situation. For example, if we had a character collider that was a cube, it would slide along the ground but could easily get caught on small protrusions. Which is why using a capsule might work better. Smart use of physics shapes will save you headaches later.

Physics engines nearly always run their own specialized version of the update step we spent so much time explaining. It's designed to be especially consistent. Recall that physics engines use rounding to keep the number of calculations manageable. We also know that when our game is working through a lot of processes at once our update and render phases (and therefore the FPS) may vary more than we'd like. If we're rounding numbers and our physics engine was subject to variations in the update time, our small rounding differences could become larger. If they continued to vary over time those rounding differences could increase dramatically. Eventually, the differences would get noticeable: rather than our cube landing a few centimeters off, it might be meters or kilometers off. Or it might fly wildly off in the wrong direction for no apparent reason. So, to avoid this physics engines usually have a separate way of handling physics to account for consistency to avoid those problems.

DIFFERENT GAME ENGINES

There are plenty of game engines to choose from and there will be more released between now (when we're writing this) and later (when you read it). But we're going to bet that Unity3D and the Unreal Engine are high on your list of engines to check out.

Unity uses C#—a special Unity flavored version of C#—which we're going to use in the following "recipe" chapters. You can find more about this in our C# recipe. Unreal, on the other hand, uses an Unreal specific C++.

Both Unity and Unreal are used by professionals and indies to create games—they have a lot of support, accessible tutorials, and are going to be fairly easy for you to download and start using. As of this writing, you can download a personal version of Unity3D for free. You can download the complete version of the Unreal Engine too, also for free.

Now, these are robust engines. They have a lot of functionality and they are geared toward use by programmers. If you're looking for something that has an interface designed with accessibility to nonprogrammers in mind, you might want to look at Gamemaker Studio or Construct.

These are also used professionally, but both are designed with non-programmers in mind. They are both 2D engines. Gamemaker Studio only runs on Windows and Construct (version 3) will be the first version of that engine to work on Mac, Windows, and Linux.

You've also got Phaser Sandbox—which runs on your browser so you don't have to download anything. It lets you make games for the web for free.

There's a lot out there—and while we don't have any affiliation with these engines, we are going to be using code written for Unity from here onwards.

Now that we have a few names floating out there, we'll look at some recommendations for how to pick your game engine.

Picking a Game Engine

You'll want to do your own research when you choose a game engine. Maybe you already have a game engine in mind. But if you aren't sure yet, let's help answer the question: Which game engine do you move forward with? They all seem awesome, they all seem like they could fit the bill.

Here's a tip and two steps to help evaluate a game engine:

The tip: Before you begin evaluating which game engine might be best suited for your project, we recommend having a game design document (GDD) or at least a strong concept in mind. You might not need to have a formalized GDD put together, but it makes the whole process of deciding on an engine go much smoother if you know what you want to do with it.

The two steps to this not-so-secret process are considering features and familiarity.

Features

When looking at a game engine it's easy to only see a list of features. That's how they are marketed and presented to us as game developers. *Automatic LOD generation*, *Effortless multiplayer integration*, etc. Try to filter those out from the beginning and focus on one: platform. A platform is where you'll eventually be able to play your game. Thinking back to our GDD or our concept, we should have what platforms we want our game to be available on figured out. This should be one of the first stops on our GDD.

Another more important factor is not just which platforms are listed, but in what order. Part of your GDD should probably also be choosing a lead platform. When it comes to games: If you try to do everything, you probably won't end up doing anything. Games are complicated endeavors and each extra platform adds a new layer of complexity. If we're trying to handle all of those complexities for every platform from the beginning, then we're going to overburden ourselves. It's almost always beneficial to choose a lead platform and develop for that first.

So how does our lead platform help us evaluate our game engine? Well, if the game engine doesn't support our lead platform we can probably nix that and look at a different engine. Another consideration is how well does a game engine support our lead platform?

If our lead platform is iOS, we want to look into the features to see how well iOS is supported. How many games have been released with this engine on iOS? It's also beneficial to look into forums and even bug reports to see how well iOS is supported—whether people had a lot of problems when targeting the platform and how the games ended up doing in the market. Check out demos or purchase a few of the games to see how they fared. If they all turn out to be laggy, then it's time to keep looking.

After looking at a lead platform, look for your secondary and other platforms to see if they are also supported. Without writing an engine from the ground up, game developers rely on a game engine for platform support. If the engine doesn't support a platform, that usually means your game won't be coming out on that platform. As we mentioned, you don't want to target all platforms at once. But once you finished your game on your lead platform, it's good to still have the option to bring your game to a new target platform without starting over with a new engine from scratch.

After you've looked at the target platform, it's time to look at other features. Keep in mind that this is where a lot of the marketing comes in to try and entice you. You'll want to keep your eye on features that will be immediately useful for your game. If you're working on a 2D game, you might not be interested in a feature like automatic normal map generation. Keeping a list of what features align with your game can help make that large list of game engines even smaller.

Another point to keep in mind is the weight of the engine. Now weight isn't an industry term, but...

If the plan is to make a simple puzzle game for PCs, almost any engine would work. Nearly all game engines support PC as a platform. In this case, Unreal Engine 4 would work. But is that the best choice? There's a lot of code to work with in that engine and a lot you'd need to pare down. Your game would have a great deal of unnecessary potential complexity to manage, and the resulting executables and resources would be quite large.

Write Once, Run Anywhere: If you hear this feature advertised on any engine, please take it with a grain of salt. The process of porting a game to multiple platforms is leaps and bounds better than it was in years past. A small indie team can port their game to a new platform in months. But the promise of writing your code once and its running everywhere is sort of a misnomer. There are engines that let you write your code once, and it runs everywhere but not equally well. A crisp 4k monitor does not function the same as a lower resolution screen on a budget phone. Your code may run on both, but you'll need to write code to handle the difference in screens. A touch screen on a mobile device is not the same as a PlayStation 4 controller; once again, you'll need to write more code to account for these differences. Sometimes when moving from one platform to another you'll need to do things like adjust the scale on the levels, or change the speed that certain characters move to make it feel better and become more suited for a new target platform. So, we tend not to consider that claim as a factor in choosing an engine.

For a project of that scope, Unreal Engine 4 might be a bit too heavy. Unity 3D is another engine we might consider, but we'll end up with a lot of the same concerns. For a small PC puzzle game, we might be better served to use something like GameMaker Studio or Construct. The features of either of these engines are a better match with the intended features of the game. And they don't have a lot of added complexity to sort through as we make a simple game.

The opposite is also true, we don't want to try to make a complex 3D game and use a very rudimentary 3D game engine. We'll want to use Unreal Engine 4 or Unity, so we can depend on a lot of the advanced 3D features to make our lives easier.

To recap: Decide what platform you want to release your game on, make a list of features you want, and compare them to the available engines and consider how complex your game is—don't go for an engine that overcomplicates a straightforward concept.

Familiarity

Basically, how comfortable are you with the game engine? The more familiar with a game engine you are, the more efficient you'll be, the better your ideas will flow, and you'll avoid pitfalls without thinking about it.

This is often why you see game developers using the same engine for subsequent projects, even if they aren't sequels. Using a game engine you're familiar with also allows you to reuse code; this can be a dangerous and slippery slope, but when used with moderation and intent it can work to your advantage.

What you'll want to do is balance familiarity with a game engine against the size of your project and what's best for your team. If you're planning for a 14 month development cycle, with half a dozen team members it's probably not the best idea to choose an engine none of you are familiar with: regardless of features, platform, and shiny marketing terms. It'd be much better to choose an engine that everyone is familiar with, or even an engine a couple of the team members are strong in.

If there's an engine you're interested in beginning to learn, start with a small project, or maybe even use it for a game jam. This allows you to start learning the basics of the engine with a game that matches your familiarity level with the complexity of the project.

> A game jam is an event—usually held over a weekend—where people try to make a working game in a short amount of time.

And if you're looking for your first game engine, then don't underestimate the power of being able to ask a friend. If you've got friends who are programmers and they're willing to lend a hand when it comes to troubleshooting—then that's something worth keeping in mind.

To recap: Don't underestimate the power of familiarity, especially when it comes to estimating the time commitments for your project. Keep in mind what engines everyone on your team is familiar with and don't commit to large complex projects on an engine without trying a smaller, manageable, and limited project with the engine first.

WRITING YOUR OWN GAME ENGINE

You may run into this argument: "If there are so many game engines out there that try to do too much, wouldn't I be better off writing one that's customized to exactly what my game needs?" And the answers are *kind of* and *no, not quite.*

Game engines are complicated programs. They need to deal with rendering, input, logic, importing models, running animations, playing sounds, and more. They have rendering libraries, physics libraries, and audio libraries you can use to avoid writing everything from the ground up.

You're still responsible for writing the *glue* between these different libraries, but those are all useful resources.

When writing your own engine, you're entirely on your own. If there are bugs to fix in the engine, it's up to you. If there are new features to add, it's up to you. If there are new platforms that didn't exist and the engine needs to be ported to them, you guessed it, you need to add them yourself.

Even if you can work past the considerations listed earlier, and decide to work on a custom engine that's suited to your game, it takes up a lot of time! Months or years can disappear into figuring out differences that only affect one platform, into optimizations that are needed to get the game to run acceptably, and into adding even small features. Any time you're building the engine, you're likely not working on your game. So a lot of time will go toward working on your engine before it's substantial enough to start working on your game in.

However

What about the "I've heard a lot of developers complain about all the issues and bugs they ran into with X engine. If they spent that time on their own engine they'd come out ahead." argument?

We totally hear this perspective as well. Just because you use a commercial engine, and the engine developers are responsible for bugs, new features and supporting new platforms, doesn't mean everything is perfect. Sometimes bugs don't get fixed and you need to write your own workarounds. Sometimes features don't work as advertised and it means you need to cut features in your own game. These are all valid concerns, but we still feel that the pros of using commercial game engines outweigh the trouble of writing your own engine—especially if the programming side of things is newer to you.

If you decide to write your own game engine, understand it will take a lot of time to get even the most basic features working. It's going to be working on a lot of engine code before you are able to work on game code. On the other hand, there is no better way of learning how a game engine works. You will touch all the major parts of a game engine and gain a better appreciation for them. And if you decide to move back to working with a commercial game engine, you'll really know what's going on under the hood.

CHAPTER 3

The Recipes

Beyond this point you'll find shorter chapters—our recipes—focusing on new programming concepts, sometimes with practical examples.

The first two recipes are similar to what we did in the Introduction to Programming, covering larger constructs in programming like classes, methods and new data types. If you're new to coding, definitely check those out first—they'll come in handy for the more specifically game-oriented recipes and it will save you from having to go backward through the book for a definition.

The other recipes are a little different. They are mostly code. There's an introduction to tell you what the code will do and some information about a programming concept that we're demonstrating—but the code will be an example of something you might actually find in a game.

ABOUT THE CODE

Throughout the code, we've included descriptions and definitions as comments in the code. Ordinarily you won't see nearly so many comments in code, but this way you can go through real code and see what's going on at the same time.

The code is also written to be understandable. Occasionally, this means that not all of the code is the most efficient. It's meant to be a learning tool, not optimized.

GAME DESIGN NOTES

As you approach programming and making your own games, it's probably a good idea to keep in mind that now not only are you trying to think like a programmer, but also like a game designer. This isn't a book that focuses on game design, and maybe you are coming from that end of the disciplinary spectrum. But in case this is also your first step into game design, let's talk (very briefly) about it.

Scope

One of the first things a lot of new designers run into is the scope of their project as measured against how long it takes to code. Programming takes time, testing, retesting, and debugging. Being good at programming means those steps take less time—but it's still a laborious process. Remember that computers are dumb. If you're programming your own game, even assuming you are using a game engine, you're still working from a mostly, gloriously blank slate! But it also means that every camera movement, every pulse of color, or other detail is yours to put in.

Put succinctly: it's a lot of work.

So start with something simple. Strip down your ideas to a core and pick a distilled and focused goal for your project. This probably isn't the project of your dreams, that game you'd make with all the resources of the world at your fingertips. But starting (and finishing!) something small and manageable will make you a better programmer, a better designer, and generally—as I'm sure you know as an artist—contribute to your sanity.

Prototyping

Keep in mind that, to start with, you probably aren't going to want to prototype with code. You're going to want to prototype with pen and paper or with a digital drawing program or with a slideshow. Prototype using a strength—know what you want to happen before you jump into trying to code it. This will give your coding experiments direction and specificity, which will help both with avoiding frustration and giving you a clear goal when you sit down to tackle the code.

When you do get to coding, know that it's not unusual for a programmer to have both the documentation for the language they are using and the game engine open while they work. In fact, we recommend it.

> Prototyping as a process looks different industry-to-industry and discipline-to-discipline. Here we're talking about making something that tests out your game or an idea for part of your game. At some point you'll want to test different things with code, but the more work you can do with a medium you're familiar with, the less frustrating the forays into code will be.

When you run into something, you're not sure about it, find it and learn it. That's really how you get better.

THE TIP OF THE ICEBERG

Hopefully the recipes that follow will answer many of your questions and speak to what you'd like to do in making a game. But there's so much more out there. And the truth is that programmers Google things. Programmers frequently aren't sure how to do something, or aren't sure if there's a better way to accomplish what they want to do. And so they Google it.

You've got an enormous resource in the Internet. Professionals use it. Indies use it. You should too. What the first two chapters of this book are geared toward is giving you a vocabulary and a mindset that will help you figure out how to phrase the question you want to ask. The following section offers answers to some of those questions. But you're going to have to venture forth eventually into the weird and wonderful world of programmers trying to effectively talk to computers.

And when you do, also remember that programmers are full of opinions about the right way to code. The truth is that there's more subjectivity to coding than might first be apparent. Worry about getting it working. Pretty is great, but it's not actually the point. And there's always more than one way to get the code working.

Finally, one of the things we found when we got into writing this book was that a lot of artists were interested in making story games or role-playing games (RPGs). If your goal is to focus more on writing a story than writing a program, then there are a lot of tools at your disposal. We've included an appendix called "Other Tools and Not Reinventing the Wheel."

HOW TO USE THE RECIPE CHAPTERS

The short version: Use these chapters in the way that makes sense to you. You can read it through from start to finish. You can flip through randomly or look at the contents to pick and choose recipes that are applicable for the game you want to make.

We recommend that you read through the first two if you are entirely new to programming. They introduce a few more simple building

Because of the size of this book, some lines of code have been forced onto two lines. We will use the "↵" character to denote when the following line belongs with the previous one as a single line of code.

blocks—concepts that will build on what we learned in Introduction to Programming. Have fun!

LIST OF RECIPES

Building Blocks

Introduction to Object-Oriented Programming

Object-Oriented Programming is a way of organizing your code. We'll talk about this as a useful tool for keeping your game code under control. We'll also cover classes (templates for objects you might want more than one of for your game) and methods (repeatable actions you can write and then reuse).

Introduction to C#

We're going to be writing in C# for the rest of the recipes—specifically in the C# you use in Unity. This recipe will introduce you to C#, to different data types (categories of information we can store and manipulate), arrays, and lists—which are ways of storing information in your game. The principles and concepts will be useful no matter what language you end up working in.

Game Recipes

Static, Singletons, and Game Managers

This recipe builds on the Introduction to Object-Oriented Programming. Static allows a piece of information or an action to be tied to the class as a whole, rather than each object you create. Singletons are a special type of class that are often used to make game managers.

Endless Runner

Here we show you how to set up an infinite runner and use character controllers for a game in 2D. We also go over inheritance—a way to use one class as a base for other classes.

Artificial Intelligence (AI) and Non-Player Characters (NPCs)

Here we cover finite state machines—a programming pattern you can use to create basic AIs, such as one might use for enemies, NPCs, and other objects the player does not control.

Physics-Based Character Controller

Here we go over creating a playable character using a physics object and getting the character to interact with their world.

CHAPTER 4

Introduction to Object-Oriented Programming

AS WE WORK ON larger and more complex programs, the amount of code involved obviously increases. Eventually the amount of code reaches a critical mass, becoming too large and too long for any one person to remember why they wrote each piece. One way to keep things manageable is using Object-Oriented Programming (OOP). OOP is a technique that we

> The OOP pillars are polymorphism, inheritance, abstraction, and encapsulation. A lot of games don't strictly adhere to OOP pillars, but if you're interested in learning more about OOP then start with researching those.

use to help divide projects up into more understandable and maintainable pieces.

In this recipe, we're going to talk about using OOP and introduce you to classes—which are a sort of template you can build and use to create multiples of the same C# object in your game.

OBJECTS

In OOP, objects are the base of everything. Since we're working with code, these aren't physical objects but rather representations of objects.

To get an idea of what we mean, let's start with physical objects and work from there. We encounter physical objects every day: a cake, a cup or a car. When we encounter these objects, we

Something to keep in mind for OOP is that it's not a game programming concept—it's a more general programming tool. So try not to think of the first examples in terms of objects in games. Once we learn how OOP works, we'll tie it back into how it works with games.

can describe them: the cake was chocolate, the cup was red, ceramic, and holds 8 ounces. The car was blue, a sedan, slightly rusted, and had a moon roof. We can also interact with everyday objects: we press the gas pedal to move the car forward and hit the brakes to slow it down.

This way of thinking about objects—in terms of their attributes and behaviors—forms the basics of how we think about objects in OOP.

In the Introduction to Programming, we looked at examples of short programs. They accomplished straightforward, simple goals. They all fit in a single screen and—most importantly—it was fairly easy to hold all of the important information you need to know about your program in your head.

But now we want to do something more complex—say you are working on a program with 200 lines of code or 600 or more? You might be able to hold all that information in your head, but it's gotten quite difficult, no? And once you start working with multiple files that all interact (and yes, you can get there!) it'll be close to impossible.

So how do programmers do it?

Well, thinking and working in objects is one way. Objects are a technique to manage the code when it starts to get out of hand. Let's talk about how objects are going to help you!

Objects are a way to categorize code. It's a way to say, this chunk of code represents this functionality. It's covering all of one portion of the project you're working on. So rather than trying to remember what order your code is in, you can look at it in chunks—objects—and you already have an idea of what it should be doing. You don't have to think about each individual line of code. We can further group the code into smaller sections by functionality. The same principle applies here as well: rather than trying to remember what each line of code in each section is, we can see how they were labeled and know how they are supposed to be used.

So, objects organize sections of code. Now for the how.

Objects possess two important characteristics: They hold states and perform behaviors. States are attributes we can describe: color, size, shape, quantity, etc. Behaviors are possible actions: calculating a total, posting a score, changing screens, and other visuals.

As an example, let's talk about a car and define some of the states and behaviors for it. Remember that we are talking about a car made of code—and not necessarily as part of a game.

So! States first! Our car might have a color, engine size, current speed, current number of passengers, maximum speed, direction, and so on. These would all be states. We use variables to store the values attached to those states. So eventually, we will have a variable holding our car object's color, engine size, current speed, etc. Note the use of the word current in that list. While several of those states are unlikely to change—like the engine size—others will change frequently—the speed or the number of passengers, for instance. When our program references this object it will need to know the current state—not the state that the object began in.

How do these states change? That would be our behaviors.

Behaviors are actions our objects can perform. Returning to our car: What are some of the common behaviors a car performs? A few might be: accelerate, decelerate, change gear, beep, and display a dashboard. These are common behaviors—pieces of functionality—which cars share. And each of these behaviors modifies a state. Accelerate will increase the speed and decelerate will decrease the speed. When these behaviors are executed, the state of our car object will change.

Now, let's take a moment to look more closely at that display dashboard behavior we snuck in there. First, why include "display dashboard" in a list of behaviors? In the real world, a car usually comes with a dashboard. But computers are dumb; we're starting from scratch (Figure 4.1). A dashboard isn't there until we program it and display it. What states would a behavior like this change? The answer is that behaviors don't always modify states. Sometimes they are an action, rather than a change to a state.

Using objects can help track what certain chunks of code do. Behaviors can be helpful this way as well. You can title a behavior using its purpose, then you'll save yourself some mental energy. You'll be able to focus on how to use the behavior, not how the behavior's code works.

FIGURE 4.1 The sum of our parts is only exactly what we put into them.

To recap: Objects are defined by states and behaviors. States define objects by tracking the variables pertinent to the object. Behaviors define actions—some of which affect states and some of which represent potential actions.

CLASSES

In programming (and software engineering), classes create the basis for objects. Classes are the blueprint or template for our objects. The name of a class should describe what type of object it will be used to create. A car class would be used for creating instances of car objects. A rocket class would be used to create instances of rockets, and an OnlineScoreboard class would be used for creating instances of online scoreboards.

All these objects have real-world equivalents—albeit a wide range of them. So what about something that only makes sense in the context of a program or game? A `HeroManager` for an RPG? Certainly!

Remember that a class only refers to the information that you've put in it. It's a template. In our example of a car, we immediately think of an entire car—but our object is only defined by the variables you've given it. These variables—the ones that will be set for each instance of your car class—can be called instance variables, fields, or instance fields; for the remainder of the book we'll use fields. You can think of them as in the fields you'd fill out on a form.

Each object comes with a number of fields that are defined in their class. Let's take a look at a simple class with some fields.

```
public class Car
{
        public int numberOfPassengers;
        private double speed;
        private int numberOfLives;
        private string color;
        private int maxSpeed;

        //… more to come
}
```

This is the skeleton to a class car. It doesn't do anything yet. It's just a template for storing information. For each new car object, we create in our program—we'll have all those fields ready. Each instance of the car class can have unique values, but the framework will be consistent.

Now let's add something else to the mix…

METHODS

Methods are the code behind our behaviors, the actions associated with an object. Adding methods to our class gives it repeatable actions—without having to rewrite code each time we want to use the behavior. The same method can receive different values and will produce results that are consistent with the values we provided.

Next, we're going to work on formatting our methods. They are written using a header and a body—which is a format you'll remember from Chapter 1.

The header defines the method's name, parameters (the values it needs to do its work), and the return value (the information it will return to us).

The body is where the action happens! It's a similar setup to pieces of code we've seen in the first chapter—you'll find the body in curly braces.

Below is an example of a method. Look for each of the three parts of the header:

```
int CalculateScore (int newPoints, int multiplier)
{
        int calculatedScore = newPoints*multiplier;
        return calculatedScore;
}
```

The example above is a method called `CalculateScore`. We can guess what that method does—it calculates a score. This method is asking for two pieces of information. The first is an integer variable called `newPoints`. The second is another integer variable called `multiplier`. These two variables—the ones in parentheses—are our parameters or method parameters.

A method can have as many parameters as we want and be named however we like (mostly). They are how we give the method the information it needs. The parameters only exist within the scope of the method body. We can use and modify them within the method body, but we can't reference them in the rest of the code. Since we want to get usable information out of the method, we have our return value. In the above example, we have `calculatedScore`. That line of code returns the variable (or value) that comes after the keyword return and sends it back to the code that called it.

Note that the variable or value returned to us must match the data type that begins the method header. Take a look at the example and you'll see that the header starts with the

> All of the methods and fields in a class are collectively called the members of a class.

data type `int`. You could also use other data types, like a `string` or boolean. You'll find a longer list of common data types in the next chapter.

What if we don't need a return value? Remember that some of our behaviors are only actions and don't alter any of our states. A method that's designed to do its work and then stop might not need to hand us any information back. In that case, instead of a data type like `int` or `string`, we'd start the method header with void. Then the method will do its work without giving us a variable or value back.

If we think back to our example of the car, we might want to make a method to `ShowDashboard()` and give it a void return value. It does its work and ends without generating new information. Other examples might include RestartLevel(), AdjustInventoryCount(), or even a ChangeDisplayLanguage() method. They are all methods that *do something*, rather than a method to *figure something out* or *find something*. When we have a *do something* method, we use a void return type since we don't need any information back after it is done.

The advantage to using a method like the one in the example is that we don't need to rewrite the same code each time we want to calculate the score, we can just call on our CalculateScore() method—simplifying our code. Also, if we have a bug somewhere in our code AND it has to do with calculating the score—then the first place to look for the problem is in the CalculateScore() method. If we rewrote the code for every circumstance when we needed to know the score, we'd be looking all over the code for our bug. So, methods also help us cut down our search from potentially thousands of lines of code when there's a problem to a single logical starting point.

Another useful point about methods is that they are easy to test and then pass to the rest of your team or coworkers. We can write dozens of methods, check them, and then give them to other people to use. Your team doesn't need to understand all the code—they can use your method names and documentation, and trust that they'll work.

Now we've gone through how methods work and how they are constructed. So how do we actually use them in code? We refer to this as calling the method.

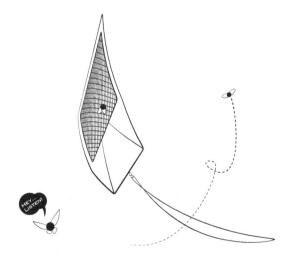

FIGURE 4.2 When it comes to finding bugs, we'll take all the help we can get!

Let's look at our `CalculateScore()` method and how we'd call it. Our header for the method was:

```
int CalculateScore(int newPoints, int multiplier)
```

Now, say we want to check the score. We need to call the method and provide it with sufficient information to answer our question. We need to provide values for the two parameters. These values must be integers, but we can plug them in as actual numbers or as variables that represent members (recall that members are all the methods and fields that make up a class). So we could say:

```
int newScore = CalculateScore (15, 30);
```

or

```
int newScore = CalculateScore(lvlPoints, combo);
```

In the first example, we've used 15 for our `newPoints` and 30 for our `multiplier`. You could use any integers here. But you're more likely to use the second example—and pull the values from different variables. In this case, both `lvlPoints` and `combo` represent integers.

Either way, the method will execute and return a value to use—and that value will then be stored and/or displayed using the variable `int newScore`.

CONSTRUCTORS

Constructors are specialized methods. In OOP, they are called when an object is created. In C# constructors share the name with the class of the object we're creating. If we have a class `car`, our constructor would be called `Car()`. Likewise, for a class called `RobotFriend`, our constructor would be called `RobotFriend()`.

Thinking back to classes, we know that they are templates for objects. We can use a class to create as many instances of an object as we need—but each object can be in any state, the variables can be holding different values, etc. So we could use class `RobotFriend()` to create a dozen robot friends all with slightly different characteristics.

Sometimes you'll want to create multiple instances of an object in succession. You could do this individually: create each object and then set the values for its fields. But that process is going to be accident prone and time consuming. It takes up a lot of code and rapidly becomes less readable. So instead, we use constructors. This combines the two steps of creating the object and setting values for its fields. We can create an object and simultaneously set a number of different values.

Let's look at an example:

```
Car vehicle1 = new Car("Yellow", 120);
```

In this example, we're creating a new car object called `vehicle1`. The part on the right is our constructor: `Car()`. It looks and functions mostly like the example of a method we saw in the previous section.

Here's a look at what's going on behind the scenes in the class:

```
Car(string color, int maxSpeed)
{
    this.color = color;
    this.maxSpeed = maxSpeed;
}
```

It looks like a method, right? This constructor is taking two parameters: (1) a `string` variable called `color` and (2) an `int` variable called `maxSpeed`. You may have noticed that we have fields that match those types and share those names in the body of the constructor. Now it's time to use the constructor and make instances of our objects!

The keyword `this` is used to refer to a member of a class. In the example, if we tried to refer to the color variable we'd only be able to access the color parameter variable—not the field variable that belongs to the class. When we use `this` we can explicitly refer to the color fields that belong to the class itself.

INSTANTIATING OBJECTS

Time to bring an object into our program and make it usable. We've learned about Object-Oriented Programming, how to set up your classes, and think about methods and behaviors. Let's put our blueprints to work.

To utilize objects we need to instantiate them. It's the same word that we use when creating variables. Here's the twist: instances of objects are stored in variables! The only difference is that the data type is the class of the object.

Here's how it looks all together with our car example:

```
Car vehicle1 = new Car("Yellow",120);
```

Let's review it piece-by-piece. The first word is `Car`, that refers to the type of the variable. It matches the class of the object we'd like to create. The next part is the name of the variable itself; here we've decided to name this first variable and the object it refers to `vehicle1`. Next is the equals sign, used as the assignment operator. On the right side of the assignment operator, we have the keyword `new`. This is a special keyword for creating instances of objects. Finally, we have this section: `Car("Yellow",120);`. This is where we're invoking the constructor for the object. This takes care of creating the instance of the object and setting up some starting values. Remember: constructors are just specialized methods. The parameters we pass to the constructor will be used or set somewhere in the creation of the object.

Now that we have an instance of an object, how do we use it? As, we like! All right, that's the end of the book folks!

Just kidding…

Now that we've created our object, we're going to want to be able to manipulate it: to change the speed—or the color—of our car if we so desire.

In order to do that, we need to talk about access modifiers. Then we'll talk about how to access and manipulate the fields of our class and call its methods!

ACCESS MODIFIERS

We've talked about members: the fields and methods that make up our classes. We know we are writing our classes as the templates to describe our objects. We might want ways to determine when and where certain code may be referenced. We have a tool called access modifiers to do exactly that. Access modifiers change how and when certain members are alterable.

We may want certain members to be accessible no matter what. We may also want to hide certain parts of the code from other classes and objects. Hiding the code means a few different things: we can avoid possible bugs, accidental edits from ourselves, or our team, and it keeps our code neat by hiding stuff we know we don't want to be changed!

This can be useful when we don't want other parts of our code to be able to change certain fields.

Access modifiers can help simplify our code as well. Say we have a class called `ScoreManager`. Say we test it, we get everything we want working, and we use access modifiers to hide all of the less relevant details. We don't need to worry about all the dozens of variables, dozens of methods, in the class; we only need to see a few relevant methods. So, instead of having dozens of members to look through we only have a handful. Below you'll find the access modifiers and what they do.

Public

`public` means that any class or object can access the member. If it's a field then any other piece of code can access the value of it, change it, or set it. This basically means *the door is wide open* for this field.

If we're talking about a method, that means that any class or object can call the method. This can be a good thing. If it's intentional, it allows us to utilize the functionality in the method freely. However, we want to avoid setting everything to `public`. It can make it seem like it might be easier, but it can lead to many bugs, more confusing and less readable code, and unintended consequences.

Private

`private` means that only the class itself can access this member. A class can modify the fields defined in itself that are marked as `private` but they are essentially invisible—they appear not to exist—from any other class. This is good for hiding and keeping fields safe from outside modification. A `private` method can only be called from within the class itself. We can still use the `private` method to simplify pieces of functionality, but they are hidden inside the class from other outside classes.

Protected

`protected` fields can be thought of as a combination of `private` and `public`. For all outside classes `protected` members still function as `private`. They are invisible, they can't be modified, they appear not to exist. However, any child classes can access `protected` fields from their parent class. We look at child and parent classes in the Endless Runner chapter.

MANIPULATING OUR OBJECTS AND THE DOT OPERATOR (.)

Members are all given access modifiers. If a member is `public`, we're able to access it from outside the object itself; in other words, we're able to access from outside the class of the object itself. If a member is `private`, we can only access it from within the class itself.

Earlier in this section, we used this example of a class called car:

```
public class Car
{
        public int numberOfPassengers;
        private double speed;
        private int numberOfLives;
        private string color;
        private int maxSpeed;

        //... more to come
}
```

If we have a `public` variable on our car object and we'd like to access the value of it we'd write something like this:

```
vehicle1.numberOfPassengers
```

This would access the number of passengers in `vehicle1`. Note that we named the instance of the object first and followed it by a period.

We use a dot operator (which is represented by a period) to access members. We know that members are the fields and methods in an object, so we can use the dot operator to access the functionality of objects. Essentially, because all instances of an object have the same members (if not with the same values), we need to specify which instance we're trying to access.

We can put that anywhere in our code we'd like to use the value, we could assign the value into another variable, print it out, or use it any other way we'd use a normal variable.

Now if we'd like to assign the value of a `public` variable we'd do the following:

```
vehicle1.numberOfPassengers = 2;
```

Remember, whatever value we're assigning to the `public` field has to match the data type that is defined for the field. `numberOfPassengers` is an `int` variable, we could store any integer there.

We can use the same format for calling methods too! Using our car object again, calling a method could look like any of these:

```
//a method with no parameters
vehicle1.StartEngine();
//a method that takes a float data type
vehicle1.Accelerate(0.7);
//a method with two parameters
vehicle.ChangeGear(4,4500);
```

Those methods are all actions and don't require a return value. If we have a method that returns a value, we can call it like so:

```
//this method will calculate the MPG then store
//the result in a variable
float currentMPG = vehicle1.CalculateMPG();
```

As long as our methods are `public`, we can call them wherever we like, give them parameters, and thus modify our objects. You can use the same format for `private` and `protected` fields, keeping in mind you've controlled where you can access those.

PROPERTIES

Properties are a third variety of information we can plug into a class. They are somewhere between a field and a method.

They are a type of member only in C# that gets and sets the value of a variable without exposing the fields.

Properties let us change variables in a consistent manner. Properties can include logic—such as checking the value being passed to a property before changing the variable behind the property. For instance, maybe we don't want a variable to have a negative value. We might want to write a property that sets our variable to zero if the value would have turned out to be less than zero.

Here's an example of that property:

```
public int Score
{
    get {return score;}
    set
    {
        if (value < 0)
        {
            score = 0;
        }
        else
        {
            score = value;
        }
    }
}
```

The get keyword is used to define the block where we return the value the property is being used to expose. The set keyword is where we can receive a value through the property and use it to modify the value of a private field.

We can also define only the get section without defining a set section. This allows us to keep the variable private, while exposing it through a read-only property. In this way, objects outside of our class can see the value of a variable, without being able to change or modify it.

THAT WAS A LOT

That's the basics of Object-Oriented Programming! You'll be able to use it in your games! We can have objects representing AIs, simulation systems, and whatever else you want! Each of these objects are self-contained bits of functionality, they can utilize and depend on other objects to model more complex behaviors. And stay organized while we do it.

CHAPTER 5

Introduction to C#

THE INTRODUCTION TO PROGRAMMING chapter was an overview of how programming languages work. Most programming languages have broad similarities: the way variables work, the programmable logic, the way that logic is implemented, etc. Now that you've got those basics, we can talk specifically about the language C# and how it operates. We'll be building off the basic concepts we laid down earlier.

This chapter includes different uses for C#, more data types, and how to use arrays and lists. This is a language that's commonly used in game development—it's what you'll use in Unity.

ABOUT C# AND UNITY

C# is a popular general-purpose Object-Oriented Programming language. C# is adaptable. It can be used for a variety of purposes: writing games, writing websites and web applications, writing business software, and research software.

Part of C#'s popularity comes from its portability. Portability is the ability of code written on one machine to run on other devices. C# runs in a kind of virtual machine. A virtual machine is a special program that can be ported to different platforms: Macs, PCs, Linux, iOS for iPhones, embedded devices like a router, or any new device that might be sold.

Formatting in C#

The formatting in C# will follow the basics of what we've covered already: each line of code executes one command, every line of code ends with a semicolon, code can be divided into blocks with curly braces, and we can create variables and name them all.

Unity

We talked about Unity in our previous chapter and it's what we're going to use for this and the other recipes that follow. Unity is a popular game engine—it's used by indies and professionals alike and you can download a version to experiment with for free. In Unity, we code with C#, but with a version of C# specific to Unity. So, instead of talking about C# generally, we're going to talk about C# in the context of Unity.

Unity Flavored C#

Okay. Now, don't panic. For what we're doing, it makes sense to focus on this subset of C# that's related to Unity. We say "flavored" because you can think of it as a spice; it's still the same dish, just more peppery. We'll learn some things that are specific to Unity and will skip over other concepts that aren't relevant to game development.

On Learning the Dark Arts of Unity

It is possible that this was the part of the book you were looking for—the part where we teach you Unity. Bad news: Unfortunately, we're not going to teach you Unity. There are entire books devoted to Unity, and we're only going to look at a few specific parts of it here. First, software changes rapidly. Between the time we write this book and the time it's published, we'd likely have outdated information. And there's not much that's more annoying than finding a tutorial and then realizing that it's obsolete.

Second, we want you to think like a programmer. And a programmer is going to check out the tutorials and content on the Unity website. That's where you'll find the most up-to-date documentation. You'll be able to learn the Unity interface there: the basics of scripting, prefabs, and a bunch of terminology. That's going to be more up-to-date than what we can give you.

Not that we aren't going to help you get started! But at this point, we also want you looking forward to how you can continue learning after you've finished this book.

Getting Started in Unity

Unity is a component-based game engine, meaning that each game object has many components. You can think about components as contained sets of functionality. Those components might include a collider component (that keeps track of when an object contacts another object), and a transform component (to track where the object is located). Components might also simulate physics, handle audio, or run scripts.

Whenever we write a script in C# in Unity, we produce a script component. Each game object can contain one or more script components (or none at all). Each script should have it's own purpose. They can be created to be reusable, accomplish specific purposes, and can communicate and utilize code between the scripts.

Methods in Unity: `Start()` and `Update()`

There are dozens of methods available in Unity, but we're going to focus on two. Each script in Unity starts out with two default methods: `Start()` and `Update()`. They both have specific purposes.

The `Start()` method sets up the object before anything begins. We can set variables, and initialize things to make sure they are ready to go before we begin. If we think back to our stage play example in Introduction to Game Engines, the `Start()` method

> Methods are a way of creating reusable sections of code and are gone over in more detail in the Introduction to Object-Oriented Programming.

happens before the curtain is drawn up for the very first time. We can use it in a number of different ways. It functions like a constructor (see the Introduction to Object-Oriented Programming) and in some cases we can use it to describe the starting state of the object. It's called once, when the object is first created.

The `Update()` method is called once every frame and runs our update step in Unity—which we covered in detail in the Introduction to Game Engines. This method is where all of our game logic lives and if you recall our stage play example, this is the set of instructions each actor follows when the curtain is down. Incrementally, each of these small changes adds up to produce the results we're looking for.

Both of these methods are set up to be called automatically on each script we write—we don't add them manually—but there are many other methods available in Unity.

To start using one of those methods we add it to our class, and it will automatically be called by Unity when it's needed.

For example, we have specialized variations of the `Update()` method like: `FixedUpdate()` and `LateUpdate()`. We can look at the Unity documentation to see exactly when and why we would need to use this special version, but they and other methods are already in Unity. We can add them to a class and they will automatically be called by Unity. Other types of methods are specialized for running when certain actions happen, when certain situations are true, or when we want to run something in the background.

Another example of a built-in method is the method `void OnCollisionEnter (Collision collision)`. This method works with the collider component. When any other object with a rigidbody component hits our object, this method is called. A temporary variable called `collision` whose data type is type `Collision` is passed in to our method where we can do specific actions on it. We can find out where it's located, we can determine what type of object we collided with, we can figure where on either object the collision happened, and even delete an object.

> When calling methods in Unity make sure the capitalization and the spelling match the definition. If either of these are off, your script probably won't throw an error. It just won't run. You can end up burning a lot of time looking in the wrong place for mistakes. So, if you have a method that's just not running, this is one of the first things we'd recommend checking.

Integrated Development Environments (IDEs)

When we're writing code in Unity, we're using an Integrated Development Environment (IDE). Back in the day, you could just open a text editor or even a command line and start writing, but as programming languages became more complicated, the editors needed to be smarter and more specifically engineered for their purpose. So, we write our code in IDEs—a specialized application for writing code.

Unity, as of this writing, supports two main IDEs: (1) MonoDevelop and (2) Visual Studio. Choosing which one you want to use is about a personal preference. No one playing your game is going to think, "Oh, I hope this wasn't written using MonoDevelop." What you probably do want to keep in mind is keeping your team on the same interface and what features you want—different IDEs will have more advanced debugging features or better autocomplete etc.

When you download Unity, you'll can also download MonoDevelop.

C# FEATURES

Now we're getting to the tofu (or meat) of our recipe. We'll explore a number of features you should be familiar with in C#.

We're going to cover data types, arrays, lists and switch statements. Data types are different categories for kinds of information—we looked at some in the Introduction to Programming. Arrays hold information and so do lists, though in slightly different ways. Switch statements are similar to `if` statements, but with a twist. You'll find more about them and their uses below.

Data Types

C# has a large number of data types you can store in variables, so this will focus on some specifically useful for Unity game programming. Below you'll find each data type, and some information about the data type (Table 5.1).

TABLE 5.1   A List of Data Types

Name	Info
int	Short for *integer*, a positive or negative number with no decimal points.
double	A number with a decimal. Calculates numbers to *a lot* of decimal places. Roughly, double the precision of a float.
float	A float is a number with a decimal that calculates to a limited number of decimal places. Typically half the storage size of a double.
bool	Short for boolean. True or false. On or off. Yes or no.
char	Short for character. Holds a single character.
string	A string of characters used to represent text.
GameObject	A Unity-specific data type to keep track of an entity that exists within a scene.
Transform	The component of a GameObject that keeps track of its location.
Vector2	A data type to track objects in 2D space using an *x* and *y* coordinate.
Vector3	A data type to track objects in 3D space using an *x*, *y* and *z* coordinate.
Quaternion	Nobody understands quaternions.
	Okay, we're joking. Mostly. They let you rotate objects in 3D space and avoid using Euler Angles. Which are subject to Gimblelock. We know that doesn't make sense—but honest to goodness programmers don't understand it either. You don't need to understand this one to use it.
Camera	A component of a GameObject that allows a viewport into the scene for rendering.
Rigidbody	A component that allows an object to have a shape, mass and frictions—letting the physics engine effect it.

Value versus Reference Types

In C#, there are two kinds of variables: Variables passed by value and variables passed by reference.

Variables passed by value mean that the code conjures up the value held in the variable before passing that information along. Variables passed by reference mean that the name of the variable is what's passed along.

You use these different sorts of variables in the same way. And you don't need to know which is which. But it can be handy information and will help you understand what's actually going on with the code that you're writing.

Arrays

Arrays are a data structure that help us organize pieces of data. The two important properties of arrays are that they have a fixed length and that everything stored in an array needs to be the same data type.

Arrays are a great way for us to organize information of a similar type! In a game, you might use an array to keep track of a character's inventory or different dialog options. You could use it to keep track of different player's positions in a racing game. As long as every piece of data is the same type of information, and we want it to have a specific order, arrays are helpful.

Look at the example below (Table 5.2):

This is an example of an array of numbers (`int` data types). The size of the array is 10, because there are 10 pieces of data that are stored in this array. When thinking about the size of an array we can think of it having a number of *slots* or locations where we can store things, almost like a single row of cubbyholes.

Arrays do not grow or shrink: they always hold the same amount of information. Arrays can hold any data type—but only that one data type in a given array. So, you might have an array of integers, an array of strings, or an array of objects. This might remind you of a spreadsheet. Which is correct! Spreadsheets are an example of a two-dimensional array (Figure 5.1). The example below is a one-dimensional array.

Arrays and lists start counting their slots from zero! The first slot of the array is 0, the second is 1, the third is 2, etc.

TABLE 5.2   A One-Dimensional Array

2	30	4	0	17	57	6	32	40	10

To initialize an array in C# we use the following format:

```
arrayType [] arrayName = new arrayType [arraySize]
```

Arrays and lists use square brackets([]). Like parentheses and curly braces there are specific places you'll see square brackets, and this is the first time we've used them in this book. When we get to lists, you'll notice that we use angled brackets(< >) as well!

FIGURE 5.1 We can also have 2-dimensional arrays—which would look something like a grid.

So, let's say we want an array of integers that has a size of 10. We'll call this array numbers. To initialize this array we'd write:

```
int [] numbers = new int [10];
```

To initialize an array of strings called names, with a size of 5 we'd write:

```
string[] names = new string [5];
```

Once you've created your array, you can start storing data in it. The slots or locations of an array are referred to by its index. By naming the array and then giving the number of the index where we want to store that specific piece of data, we store data in the array. If you look back to our first array, numbers, we can store the value 14 in the second slot of the array by writing the following:

```
numbers [1] = 14;
```

Note that the second place in the array is called 1, because arrays start counting from zero. This is similar to storing a value in a variable. The difference is that we give the data a number, indicating the index where we're storing that value.

If we want to place multiple pieces of information into an array at once when it is created, we could write it like so:

```
int [] array = new int [5] {1, 3, 3, 4, 3};
```

Getting the value from an array is just as easy:

```
Debug.Log (numbers [1]);
```

This would return the number stored in the second location to the debug menu in Unity.

If we need to get the size (or length) of an array we can access it by using the dot operator (.) and the Length property.

```
//print out the array's
//length, which is 10 here
Debug.Log (numbers.Length)
```

Debug.Log() is a command we can use to print useful information to Unity's console. This is helpful for figuring out what is happening in the code when we can't tell just by looking at the screen.

You'll always need to use the brackets along with the index of the location you're selecting when you look at the value in an array.

If we want to visit every item in an array we can use our old friend the for loop! That would look like this:

```
for(int i = 0; i < numbers.length; i++)
{
    //this code will visit every number in our array
    //of ints, increment each and print each
    numbers[1]++;
    Debug.Log(numbers[i]);
}
```

Among other things, we can use the loop to modify every value, or access every value.

If we have a situation where we need to quickly print out every value of an array we can use the nifty `foreach` loop like this:

```
    foreach(int value in numbers)
    {
    Debug.Log(value);
}
```

That's an overview of arrays in C#! To review: In order to use an array, you have to create one first. To do so, you'll need to know what data type you'd like to store and how many slots for information you need.

> A `foreach` loop will perform the loop for each piece of information in a set of data—in this case, it will perform the loop for each slot in the array.

Then you can start storing information in the array. We can check to see what information is in a given slot and use a loop to access each slot in an array in order.

Switch

Switch statements are a type of conditional statement. They mimic the structure of an `if-else...if-else` statement, but allow us to use much less code. Switch statements are typically used with `int` or `string` data types. Switch statements aren't designed to match a range of values, but rather match specific cases.

```
switch(variable)
{
```

```
        case 1:
                //case one was matched
                break;

        case 2:
                //case two was matched
                //We can have as many lines in a case.
                //It's ended with a break;
                break;

        Default:
                //This will run when no cases are
                //matched
        break;
}
```

A switch statement starts out with the keyword switch, followed by the condition in the parentheses, then the body of the switch statement. We put the variable we want to evaluate in the parentheses. So far this is similar to an if statement. But rather than doing the comparison in the parentheses we do switch statement comparisons with a case statement in the body of the switch.

Each case starts the keyword case. Next, we have the value we are looking for in that case. In the previous example, the first case is looking for a 1. After the value, start the body of the case with a colon. When that case is matched, it will run the body of that case. The body of each case is ended with a break;.

We have the option of including a Default case that will run if none of the cases are matched. The Default case comes last, starts with the default keyword, and is ended with break;.

Lists

Lists are similar to arrays. Like arrays, all of the items in a list need to be of the same data type. Unlike arrays, lists can store any amount of information—rather than the fixed number in an array. A list changes size, depending on how many items are in it.

Rather than thinking about a set of cubbyholes with a fixed size, we can think of a list as a train, where each train car stores one item. Each item lives in one car. As we need more space, we can add more items by connecting a new car to the end of the train or by adding one in the middle or at the beginning.

We can also access the data stored in lists and modify them. Let's take a look at the syntax for how we create and use lists.

The way we create a list is fairly different from how we create an array. Here's the basic format:

```
List<datatype> listname = new List<datatype>();
```

Each time we use the keyword `list` we need to tell the list what data type it contains. Whether it be `int`s, `GameObjects`, `Transforms`, or `strings`: we need to specify a type. If we'd like to declare a list of `int`s, called `numbers2` we could do it like so:

```
List<int> numbers2 = new List<int>();
```

Recall that we don't need to specify a size for our list. When we create our list, it starts out with a size of zero. When we need to access the size (and see how big it's gotten) we can do so by using the name of the list, the dot operator, and the `Count` property. Like so:

```
//This will print out the size of the list: zero
Debug.Log(numbers2.Count);
```

To add something to our list we can use the `method.Add()`. We just need to provide a variable or a value that matches the data type defined for our list. So, if we'd like to add the numbers 1 through 5 to our list, we write the following:

```
numbers2.Add(1);
numbers2.Add(2);
numbers2.Add(3);
numbers2.Add(4);
numbers2.Add(5);
//This will print out the size of the list: five
Debug.Log(numbers2.Count);
```

If you're creating your list and know what you'd like to put in it, then you can add values all at once, instead of one at a time. To do this, use this format:

```
List<int> numbers2 = new List<int>() {1, 2, 3, 4, 5};
```

Pretty simple! Practically speaking there is no limit to how many items we can add to lists.

However, lists are slower to use than arrays, so if we need to add and remove hundreds of items from a data structure very quickly, an array might be a better choice. Lists also take up more space in memory than an array, so if there is a lot of data to store, an array is better.

There are a handful of other methods for lists that are worth mentioning. We're going to run through them fast, to give you an idea of what's possible. We'll use our `numbers2` list as an example. Ready?

This method finds and removes an item from a list:

```
numbers2.Remove(itemToRemove);
```

This one removes an item from a specific index in the list. In this case, the fourth index. Remember that we count from zero in lists.

```
numbers2.RemoveAt(3);
```

This will empty the list:

```
numbers2.Clear();
```

This will check to see if an item exists in a list:

```
numbers2.Contains(item);
```

This will sort the items in a list. By default, it will sort numerical data in ascending order or strings in alphabetical order.

```
number2.Sort();
```

This method will look for where a certain piece of data is stored and return the index.

```
numbers2.IndexOf(item);
```

If we wanted to use a list to make a new array, we could write it like this:

```
int[] newArray = numbers2.ToArray();
```

Note that the array will use the length of the list as the length of the array created, so in this case you don't have to specify how long `newArray` would be!

THAT'S IT!

Data types, arrays, switch statements, and lists are all versatile tools for you to use in your programming. While this recipe is specifically using the methods and formatting used in Unity's version of C#, the concepts will translate fairly closely into other programming languages.

CHAPTER 6

Static, Singletons, and Game Managers

A S YOUR GAME GROWS, you're going to want tools to keep it under control. Remember our cardinal rule that programmers are lazy? If it's possible to do something once, then we do it once. This also means that there are fewer places to check for bugs.

Static, singletons, and game managers are all tools to help keep your code under control. They help create reusable systems—things that you want to be available to you in multiple levels, and throughout your game.

STATIC

We can use the keyword `static` in our code to let to let members—fields, properties, and methods—be available and shared across a class. It ties the members to the template, rather than to the objects (the instances of the classes).

Let's dig into that one a little more, shall we?

Say we had a class `RobotFriend`. Inside the class, we might have fields to keep track of the name, the speed, the color, etc., but we have a situation where we might need to figure out how many robot friends in total we have. We could try to make a field called `int numberOfRobot Friends` to keep track of the number of `RobotFriend` instances, but it will run into problems and not work as intended—because it would be stored multiple times: in each instance of `RobotFriend` we create. So, once we add one RobotFriend, we'll need to find every other RobotFriend and update the variable representing the total number of `RobotFriend` instances. We'll need to keep updating that variable in each RobotFriend. If we miss one of those, our variable won't hold the proper value.

So instead, we use that same variable but put static out in front, like so:

```
private static numberOfRobotFriends
```

The designation `static` means that this no longer belongs to any one instance of our `RobotFriend`, but rather with the `RobotFriend` class as a whole and is shared amongst all `RobotFriend` objects regardless of when they are created. So now, when we create a new `RobotFriend` instance, we can have it update the static `numberOfRobotFriend` variable. When we do, all RobotFriend instances share the static variable, and the number is accurately represented in each instance. No need to manage multiple variables here and there or make sure that all the `RobotFriend` objects saw the update: static allows members to be shared across all instances of a class.

> The private keyword used here is an access modifier and you can find more about it in the Introduction to Object-Oriented Programming recipe.

We can also mark methods as static. Ordinarily, in order to call a method we need to create an instance of the class first. If we mark a method as static, we can still call it from within an instance of a class but now we also have the ability to call the method without creating an individual instance first. This can be useful when we have a static variable that we might want to use in a constructor when creating all instances of an object. If we want to run some sort of calculation on the static variable before we start creating instances we can't use a normal method. This is where we can use a static method.

For example: we might want a static variable `currentObjective` to track what the collective objective of our robot friends is. Our `RobotFriend` instances will use the variable to track their objective but before we create our first `RobotFriend` we can use the variable to set what their objective will be. We can call a static method `RobotFriend.determineCurrentObjective();` to find out what the current objective is and store it in the `currentObjective` static variable.

Static methods can accept input parameters, change static variables, and return values. We talk about methods in more detail in the Introduction to Object-Oriented Programming chapter if you need a refresher.

SINGLETONS AND GAME MANAGERS

Singletons are a special way of designing a class. They should be used sparingly. A singleton is used to create a class that can only have one instance at a time. It's useful for things like keeping track of information needed in multiple levels or running music in a game—you don't want to have different code controlling when music is running, since it could overlap in unexpected and annoying ways.

Game managers are a kind of singleton that we use in games. They are a game programming design pattern used to create an object to manage state, functionality, and information across levels. Unfortunately, they have a bad reputation for being poorly implemented, overused, and encouraging poor design. Like anything, it's in how you use it! Getting into the virtues of one stance or the other is outside the scope of this book and there's a plethora of information on both sides available on the Internet.

Just keep in mind that game managers should be as small and concise as possible. They shouldn't contain more functionality than is necessary and if individual objects or classes can take care of storing and managing the functionality, than it probably doesn't belong in a game manager.

We only want one instance of a game manager in our game at any given time. We can imagine the chaos in our game world if we ended up with two high scores—both valid and invalid—or if one game manager decided to go to the main menu while the other decided to go to level 3. So in order to ensure that there is only one instance in a scene, we can follow the singleton pattern. Which, recall, is a specific way of designing classes—and in our case, a game manager—to where only one instance can exist.

A game manager is a place where we can store information we might need in multiple places, allows us to carry information from one level to another, and hold information that isn't specific to any level. Things like the player's score, what levels they've unlocked, and saving the game might be the sort of information and functionality you want in your game manager.

IN THE CODE

In this recipe, we'll create a game manager that can keep track of information such as: what state the game is in, information that needs to persist across levels such as current score, or a difficulty setting. It provides a convenient place to perform actions that every level might need—like saving.

PROJECT SETUP

For this recipe, there's not much we need to do to get things set up. First, we need to place an empty game object in our hierarchy and name it GameManager. Next, we need to create a new C# script called GameManager and add the following code to it. Note: When creating a new C# script we do not need to add the *.cs* to the end of it, that's added automatically.

```
-------------------GameManager.cs-------------------

//need to add for BinaryFormatter
using System;
using System.Collections;
using System.Collections.Generic;
//need to add for FileStream
using System.IO;
using System.Runtime.Serialization.Formatters.Binary;
using UnityEngine;

public class GameManager : MonoBehaviour
{
    //create a static variable we can use to track this
    //the single instance
    private static GameManager instance = null;
    // this is where we can add any variables we want
    //to track in our game manager
    public float score;

    //as soon as the object is active
    private void Awake()
    {
        //if a game manager isn't stored in the static
        //field yet we need to set one
        if (instance == null)
        {
            //store the current instance
            instance = this;
            //when we are changing scenes, insure our
            //game manager persists
            DontDestroyOnLoad(this.gameObject);
        }
        else
```

```
    {
        //if a game manager is already stored in the
        //static field we don't need a new one
        Destroy(this.gameObject);
    }
}

//a public property so we can retrieve instances of
//our game manager
public static GameManager Instance
{
    get
    { //if a game manager is not set on a game object
      if (instance == null)
      {
          //create a new game object
          GameObject gm = new GameObject ⏎
          ("GameManager");
          //and attach a game manager to it
          instance = gm.AddComponent<GameManager>();
      }
      //return the game manager through the
      //property
      return instance;
    }
}

//a default constructor for our game manager
protected GameManager()
{

}

// we can use the update method if there's any
//logic our game manager needs
void Update()
{

//we can use the s and l keys to save and
//load our game. in a real game we would
//replace these with specific methods
//to perform those actions
```

```
   if (Input.GetKey("s"))
   {
    GameManager.Instance.SaveGame("savegame.dat");
   }
   if (Input.GetKey("l"))
   {
    GameManager.Instance.LoadGame("loadgame.dat");
   }
}

//we can use this space to add methods to our game
//manager

//public method that takes a file name for saving
//games
public void SaveGame(string fileName)
{
    //we need to use a binary formatter to serialize
    //the save file
    BinaryFormatter bf = new BinaryFormatter();
    //the file steam lets us write to a file
    FileStream fs = File.Create(Application. ↵
    persistentDataPath + fileName);

    //here we can settle values that we want stored
    //in the saved file
    SaveRecord newSaveFile = new SaveRecord();
    //set the values in the file before saving
    newSaveFile.score = this.score;

    Debug.Log("Saving : " + newSaveFile.score);

    //serialize and save the file
    bf.Serialize(fs, newSaveFile);
    //don't forget to close the filestream!
    fs.Close();
}

public void LoadGame(string fileName)
{
    //we need to use a binary formatter to
    //deserialize the save file
    BinaryFormatter bf = new BinaryFormatter();
```

```
        //the filestream lets us read from a file
        FileStream fs = File.Open(Application. ↵
        persistentDataPath + fileName, FileMode.Open);

        //here we are deserializing a file, they casting
        //it to a SaveRecord object
        SaveRecord SaveFile = (SaveRecord)
        bf.Deserialize(fs);

        Debug.Log("Loaded : " + SaveFile.score);

        //we can take the code from the deserialized
        //file and populate our game manager with it
        this.score = SaveFile.score;
        //don't forget to close the filestream!
        fs.Close();
    }

}


//We need this attribute to enable our SaveRecord
//class to be able to be serialized
[Serializable]
//This class represents the info we want to be saved
//in our save file
public class SaveRecord
{
    //add any variables that should be written to our
    //save file here
    public float score;
}
```

After we're done writing the GameManager.cs script, we can add the
script as a script component to our GameManager game object in the
hierarchy by dragging and dropping the script on it. And that's it! It should
look like Figure 6.1.

To verify everything is working correctly, when we start our game we
should see the GameManager object move in the hierarchy to a section

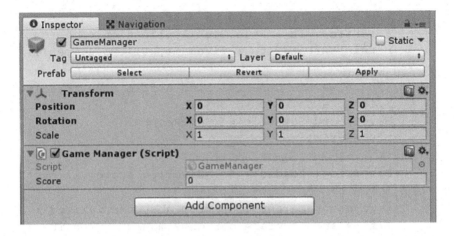

FIGURE 6.1 Our game manager script is attached to our game manager object.

FIGURE 6.2 When our game manager is in the DontDestroyOnLoad section it will persist across levels.

called *DontDestroyOnLoad* (Figure 6.2). This means our `GameManager` will persist when we move throughout levels. In order to track more variables in our `GameManager` we just need to add them as a field, like the variable `score` we already added.

To use the `GameManager` we just need to reference it in one of our other scripts like the following:

```
GameManager.Instance.score++;
```

This would allow us to cause our score to go up. We could add that anywhere in our game where something would need to make the score go up. For testing purposes we've added some code to the `Update()` method in our `GameManager` that allows us to save our game to a file by pressing the *s* key and to load our game by pressing the *l* key. You wouldn't want to leave that functionality in a full game.

We'll explore using the game manager more in our next recipe.

CHAPTER 7

Endless Runner

Iᴺ ᴛʜɪs ᴄʜᴀᴘᴛᴇʀ ᴡᴇ ᴡɪʟʟ ʙᴇ building an infinite runner type game. To do this, we'll explore using an Object-Oriented Programming (OOP) technique called inheritance and look at how character controllers work in Unity before getting into the code.

INHERITANCE, PARENT CLASSES, AND CHILD CLASSES

Inheritance is an OOP technique that allows us to make our code more usable, reduce complexity, and help us repeat useful functionality. Inheritance allows classes to potentially utilize fields and methods defined in another class.

Say we have a class `vehicle`. We have the field's `maximumSpeed`, `numberOfPassengers`, and `numberOfWheels`. This vehicle class also has these methods: `move()`, `stop()`, and `turn()`.

Now, say we want to make a class `car`, we could create it separately, but we can imagine that it might share a lot of the same fields and methods with our vehicle class. In addition, if we had a motorcycle, helicopter, and boat classes—they would also share some common methods and fields

All the default classes created by Unity inherit from something called MonoBehaviour. This is the base class that allows all Unity scripts to have access to a set of standard Unity variables and methods. This is how Unity knows to automatically call the `Start()`, `Update()` or whatever other Unity methods we add—this is just to help you understand how Unity is set up to work, not something you need to worry about in your code!

amongst all vehicles. Without using inheritance, we'd be forced to rewrite those same fields and methods for each of those classes. Any time there is a change to the way one of those methods functions, we'd need to change it in each individual class.

With inheritance, we can have each of our new classes inherit from the Vehicle class by using the following syntax:

A parent class can be also be called a superclass or a base class. A child class can be also be called a subclass or derived class. All these terms are interchangeable.

```
public class Car: Vehicle
{
    //class body goes here
}
```

Any variables or methods that are marked public—available for any class to modify—or protected—available for any child class to modify—will be available for the child class to use. The child class can modify and utilize those variables and methods as if that code was written in the new class in the first place. Additionally, each child class is able to add their own new fields and methods. These will exist only in the child class and won't effect the parent class in any way.

In C# classes can only inherit from one parent class.

We can have a parent class Vehicle and have our child classes car, motorcycle, helicopter, and boat each inherit from it. This means they have access to the protected or public variables and methods. A big advantage to this is that if we need to change the way a method functions, such as the move() method, we modify it in the parent class Vehicle and that change will affect all the classes inheriting from it.

Overriding

We might also run into a situation where we want to utilize nearly all of the functionality in a parent class but a specific method doesn't work for a child class. If we think about our example, the helicopter is the only one that doesn't travel along the surface of something. The move() method in the vehicle class would be sufficient for all the vehicles that move on a surface, but for the helicopter we may need to take into account the altitude. With inheritance, if the parent class marks a method with the `virtual` keyword, it's giving any child classes the option to provide their own more specialized version of a method. You'll see an example of this in the code later.

The process of providing a more specialized version of an inherited method is called overriding. So our helicopter will want to override the `move ()` method inherited from the vehicle class with its own specialized version suited to its purposes.

A Few Final Details on Inheritance

When we're looking in the code of a child class, we will only see the code for the child class. It is important to remember that even though we can't see the fields and methods, they are still a part of the child class. This let's us add functionality specific to our child classes, without adding more code into a single file! This can help us organize our code, because we know only the code that belongs to that class will appear. So, if we need to look for a specific bit of functionality we know where to find it.

There's no limit on the number of classes we can have in an inheritance hierarchy. If we want to add a class `Sedan` to inherit from `Car`, we can do that. But we want to make sure we are careful, only creating subclasses where necessary.

CHARACTER CONTROLLERS

In order to move our characters, we'll be using Unity's character controller class. The character controller class is a set of convenient methods, functionality, and shortcuts that allow us to move characters around. We can write our own character controllers from scratch, but there are dozens of edge cases and special situations and functionalities we would need to program by hand. Classes like these are important because characters don't always follow the same physics rules as the rest of the game.

For example: in a game when your character is running and changes directions, the character stops and turns immediately. If we were using realistic physics with our character, they would need to slow down and then turn. But when you use those realistic physics in a game, the character reactions might seem laggy and players may feel like they are not in complete control of the character.

We can make our own character controller or use the ones already built into Unity! As we said, for this recipe we're going to use Unity's character controllers.

The character controller has its own special kind of physics built in. It also takes care of figuring out if a character is standing on the ground—which may seem like a simple thing to determine. But in a game world, it's actually a fairly complicated calculation involving dozens of edge cases.

Because character controllers have their own set of special physics, they don't interact with the physics objects in Unity. In order to have a character that interacts with physics, we need to have it based on a physics object and not a character controller. We'll explore that in the Physics-Based Character Controller.

Object Pooling

In this recipe we will also cover simple object pooling, which is a way to make your games more efficient. Oftentimes in games we'll need to reuse the same game object multiple times throughout a level. Constantly creating and destroying instances of the game object takes processing power—so instead we can send it to a *waiting room* when we want to and bring it back in play when needed.

Base

In a child class, we may find instances where we might need to call a method in our parent class. We can use the base keyword to represent our parent class. Using the dot operator allows us to access and use any method in the parent class our current child class has inherited from.

IN THE CODE

In this recipe, we'll be creating an infinite runner with multiple characters. We'll have a base class that all of our individual characters will inherit from. And we'll show how to utilize the parent class's fields in our child classes to customize each of the characters.

PROJECT SETUP

This recipe has a number of different small steps, so be sure to read through this carefully.

To begin, let's add a new cube to our hierarchy named *Platform* and set its size to (8, 0.5, 3). Let's give it the tag *Platform* and finally let's add a

▼ 🏂 **Rigidbody**		🔲 ✿.
Mass	1	
Drag	0	
Angular Drag	0.05	
Use Gravity	☐	
Is Kinematic	☑	
Interpolate	None	⬍
Collision Detection	Discrete	⬍
▶ Constraints		

FIGURE 7.1 "Is Kinematic" means forces won't affect this rigid body—things like gravity. That way our platform *won't* plummet from the sky.

rigidbody component to it. We'll want to enable the *Is Kinematic* option on the rigidbody (Figure 7.1). We place our platform at position (2.5, 0, 0). We'll then want to drag our *Platform* from our hierarchy to our project panel so we can create a Prefab.

Next let's add our players. We will be naming them *Person, Kangaroo*, and *FlyingSquirrel*. For the Person, we used a capsule, for the Kangaroo we used a cube with an orangish material, and for the Flying Squirrel we flattened out another cube and used a blue material. When you're working on your own game replace these with your own models!

Arrange all of the players onto the platform and add one Character-Controller component to `Person`, `Kangaroo`, and `FlyingSquirrel`. We have them set up as in Figure 7.2.

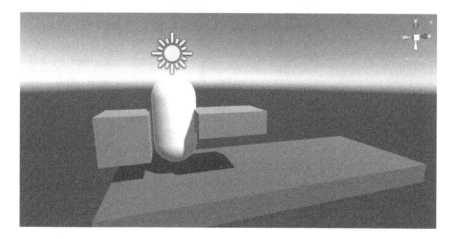

FIGURE 7.2 A screenshot.

Next we will want to create a new C# script called *Player*. We will add the following code so all of our players can inherit from it:

```csharp
---------------------------Player.cs-------------------------
using System;
using System.Collections;
using System.Collections.Generic;
using UnityEngine;

public class Player : MonoBehaviour
{
    //any child classes can access public variables
    public float speed = 3f;
    public float gravity = 15f;
    public float jumpStrength = 8f;
    protected Vector3 movement = Vector3.zero;
    //this is a shortcut for: new Vector3(0f, 0f, 0f);
    protected Vector3 movement = Vector3.zero;

    //we use the access modifier protected so any child
    //classes can access and modify this variable
    protected CharacterController controller;

    void Start()
    {
        //save the reference to our character controller
        controller = GetComponent<CharacterController>();
    }


    protected virtual void Update()
    {

        //we can calculate the new x position to keep our
        //character running
        float newX = transform.position.x + speed * Time.↲
        deltaTime;
```

```
//then let's move our character
transform.position = new Vector3(newX, transform.↵
position.y, transform.position.z);

//first we'll check if we're on the ground, then let's
//check to see if the jump button was button was
//pressed
if (controller.isGrounded && Input.↵
GetButton("Jump"))
{
  //we apply the jump force
  movement.y = jumpStrength;
}
//if we are in the air we want gravity
//to pull us downward
if (!controller.isGrounded)
{
  movement.y -= gravity * Time.deltaTime;
}

//once we have applied all the forces to our
//movement vector we call the move method to
//simulate it
  controller.Move(movement * Time.deltaTime);
  }
}
```

Once you're finished with this script you can add three more C# scripts called Person, Kangaroo, and FlyingSquirrel. Add the respective code to each of those scripts.

```
----------------------Person.cs----------------------
using System.Collections;
using System.Collections.Generic;
using UnityEngine;

public class Person : Player
{
```

```
    //we can use this space to add new fields to this
    //class

    // Use this for initialization
    void Start()
    {
      //we still need to set our controller
      controller = GetComponent<CharacterController>();
    }

    //we can use this space to add new methods to this
    //class
}


---------------------Kangaroo.cs---------------------
using System.Collections;
using System.Collections.Generic;

using UnityEngine;
public class Kangaroo : Player
{

  //we can use this space to add new fields to this
  //class
  // Use this for initialization
  void Start()
  {
    //our kangaroo specific values
    jumpStrength = 20f;
    //we still need to set our controller
    controller = GetComponent<CharacterController>();
  }

  //we can use this space to add new methods to this
  //class

}
```

```
-------------------FlyingSquirrel.cs----------------
using System.Collections;
using System.Collections.Generic;
using UnityEngine;

public class FlyingSquirrel : Player
{
  //we can use this space to add new fields to this
  //class
  public float dropSpeed = 25f;

  // Use this for initialization
  void Start()
  {
    //our flying squirrel specific values
    gravity = 3f;
    //we still need to set our controller
    controller = GetComponent<CharacterController>();
  }

  //we can use this space to add new methods to this
  //class

  // the version of update we inherited isn't
  //specific enough so we use the "override" keyword to
  //make our own in the child class
  protected override void Update()
  {

    //we can calculate the new x position to keep our
    //character running
    float newX = transform.position.x + speed * Time.⏎
    deltaTime;

    //then let's move our character
    transform.position = new Vector3(newX, transform.⏎
    position.y, transform.position.z);
```

```
  //when our squirrel is on the ground reset the
  //floaty gravity
  if (controller.isGrounded)
  {
    gravity = 3f;
  }
  //when we are in the air
  else
  {
    //and press the jump button, trigger a drop by
    //increasing the gravity
    if (Input.GetButton("Jump"))
    {
      gravity = dropSpeed;
    }
    //if we are in the air we want gravity to
    //pull us down
    movement.y -= gravity * Time.deltaTime;
  }

  //once we have applied all the forces to our
  //movement vector we call the move method to
  //simulate it
  controller.Move(movement * Time.deltaTime);


}


}
```

After writing those scripts add the `Person` script to the Person game object, the `Kangaroo` script to our Kangaroo game object, and our `FlyingSquirrel` script to our Flying Squirrel game object (Figure 7.3).

Now we have characters. But they're all on screen at the same time, and our camera doesn't follow them. Let's fix both of those problems next.

Create a new C# script called `CameraMover`. We can add it to our Main Camera then add the following code:

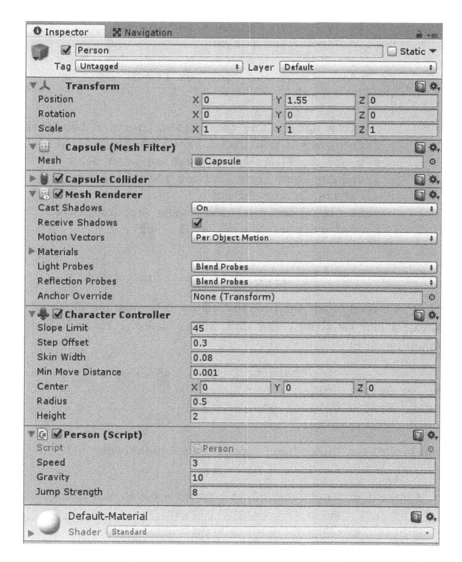

FIGURE 7.3   Our Person game object has these components.

```
--------------------CameraMover.cs--------------------
using System.Collections;
using System.Collections.Generic;
using UnityEngine;

public class CameraMover : MonoBehaviour
{
```

```
        //this is how we'll track our player
        public GameObject player;

        // Update is called once per frame
        void Update()
        {
          //let's update the camera's x position based on
          //the player position. we've hardcoded the
          //y and z values here, meaning we'd need to
          //update them here, rather than move the
          //camera in the editor
          this.transform.position = new Vector3(player.↵
          transform.position.x, 4.5f, -8f);
        }
}
```

Now we'll want to add the code that allows us to swap our characters.
Create a new C# script called CharacterSwapper.cs and all the
following code:

```
-----------------CharacterSwapper.cs-------------------
using System.Collections;
using System.Collections.Generic;
using UnityEngine;

public class CharacterSwapper : MonoBehaviour
{

  //store an instance of the camera mover script so
  //we can change the target player
  public CameraMover cameraMover;

  //this variable keeps track of the current character
  public int currentCharacter = 0;

  //an array to hold all of our characters
  public GameObject[] characters;

  //Use this for initialization
  void Start()
  {
```

```
  //we want to run this on start to disable all but
  //the current character
    ChangeCharacter(currentCharacter);
}
// Update is called once per frame
void Update()
{
    GameManager.Instance.score += Time.deltaTime;


    //change to a person
    if (Input.GetKey("1"))
    {
        ChangeCharacter(0);
    }
    //change to a kangaroo
    else if (Input.GetKey("2"))
    {
        ChangeCharacter(1);
    }
    //change to a flying squirrel
    else if (Input.GetKey("3"))
    {
        ChangeCharacter(2);
    }
}


//our method to change the character. it takes an
//int which represents the new character
private void ChangeCharacter(int newCharacter)
{
  //before we change the character, this stores the
  //current position so we can move the new character
  //there
  Vector3 tempPosition = characters[current ⏎
  Character].transform.position;

    //changes the character
    currentCharacter = newCharacter;
```

```
//let's look through every character in our array
//for (int i = 0; i < characters.Length; i++)
{
  //if we're at the current character, let's
  //make sure they're active, then move them to
  //the stored position
   if (i == currentCharacter)
   {
       characters[i].SetActive(true);
       characters[i].transform.position = ⏎
       tempPosition;

   }
   //if it's not the current character let's
   //make sure that are inactive
   else
   {
       characters[i].SetActive(false);
   }
}
//finally let's not forget to update the player
//that the camera is looking at
cameraMover.player = characters[currentCharacter];

  }
}
```

After we've completed the CharacterSwapper script, we'll need to add it as a script component to our Main Camera.

At this point we should have our CameraMover and CharacterSwapper scripts on our Main Camera. Now we want to populate the references in our scripts with our actual game objects. This way when our scripts are trying to reference them it knows which game objects we are referring to.

With our Main Camera selected we will want to drag the Person game object from the hierarchy onto the Player field in the CameraMover script component. Next on the CharacterSwapper we can expand the Character's field and we will want to set the Character's array to size 3. Now you can drag the Person, Kangaroo, and FlyingSquirrel game objects from our hierarchy into the three slots in that order. It should look like Figure 7.4.

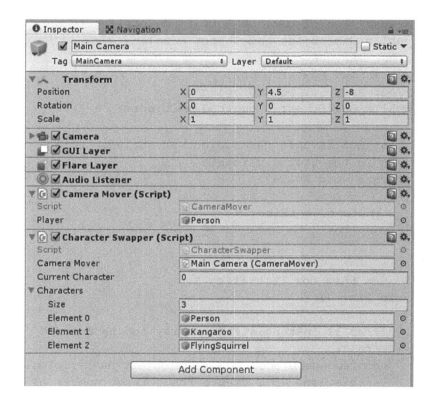

FIGURE 7.4   Be sure to set the character array to 3 so that we can have our 3 characters.

Now we need to create our script responsible for our platform object pool. Create a new C# script called ObjectPool and add the following code:

```
-------------------ObjectPool.cs--------------------

using System.Collections;
using System.Collections.Generic;
using UnityEngine;



public class ObjectPool : MonoBehaviour
{

  //create a static variable we can use to reference
  //this object
  public static ObjectPool instance;
```

```
//what type of game object are we pooling
public GameObject gameObjectToPool;
//how many game objects
public int numberToPool;
//our array of pooled objects
public GameObject[] pooledGameObjects;


//as soon as this game object is active, store
//it in the static variable
private void Awake()
{
    instance = this;
}



// Use this for initialization
void Start()
{
    //we'll instantiate our array to the desired
    //size
    pooledGameObjects = new GameObject[numberToPool];
    //this loop will create the correct number of
    //objects in the pool and make sure they are all
    //inactive
    for (int i = 0; i < numberToPool; i++)
    {
        GameObject newObj = (GameObject) ↵
        Instantiate(gameObjectToPool);
        newObj.SetActive(false);
        pooledGameObjects[i] = newObj;
    }
}


//we call this method when we need an object from
//the pool
public GameObject GetObjectFromPool()
{
    //we will loop through the pool and find an
    //inactive object
    for (int i = 0; i < pooledGameObjects.Length; ↵
    i++)
```

```
    {
        //when we find an inactive object
        //return it
        if (!pooledGameObjects[i].activeInHierarchy)
        {
            return pooledGameObjects[i];
        }
    }
    //if we go all the way through the loop without
    //returning, it means there are no currently
    //inactive objects so we return null
    return null;
}

}
```

Now we will want to create two new game objects as children of our *MainCamera* in the hierarchy. So let's create a new Cube game object, name camera `Deactivater`, then make sure it's a child of our Main Camera by dragging and dropping it on the camera. Let's move it to position (−30, 0, 8) (Figure 7.5). Next, under the Box Collider component we will want to change the size to (3, 20, 10) and also set the *Is Trigger* option to yes. It should look like Figure 7.6.

Now let's add a new C# script called `Deactivater`, add it to our `Deactivater` game object, and add the following code to it:

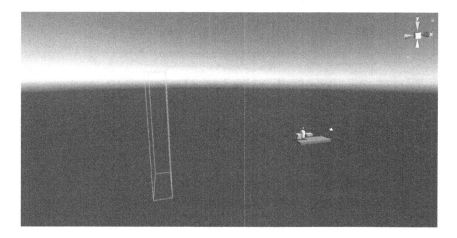

FIGURE 7.5 Our deactivator should be out of view of the camera—so that the player doesn't see the platforms disappearing.

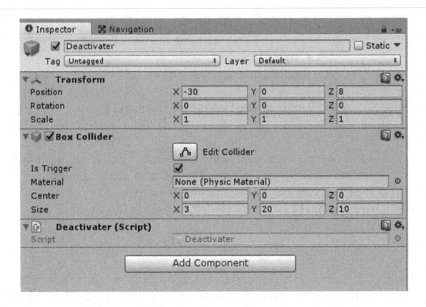

FIGURE 7.6 Enabling "Is Trigger" means the object isn't solid.

```
-------------------Deactivater.cs-------------------
using System.Collections;
using System.Collections.Generic;
using UnityEngine;

public class Deactivater : MonoBehaviour
{

  //when we intersect with the trigger
  private void OnTriggerEnter(Collider other)
  {
      //check if the object has the tag 'platform'
      if (other.CompareTag("Platform"))
      {
        //deactivate the platform
        other.gameObject.SetActive(false);
      }
  }
}
-----------------------------------------------------
```

Next we want to create a new *Empty* game object and name it Spawner. We will want to move our spawner off to the right. Ours is about at position (14,–2,0). Let's create a new C# script called Spawner, and add it to our spawner game object. Now you can add the following code to the new script:

```
-------------------------Spawner.cs---------------------
using System.Collections;
using System.Collections.Generic;
using UnityEngine;

public class Spawner : MonoBehaviour
{

  //what's the shortest time in seconds we'd want to
  //drop a platform
  public float minimumDropTime = 2f;
  //what's the longest time in seconds we'd want to
  //drop a platform
  public float maximumDropTime = 4f;

  //how high above or below the platform spawner do
  //we want to place new platforms
  public float placementDistanceRange = 3f;
  //this timer will keep track of our time until next
  //the spawn
  private float timer = 0f;


  // Use this for initialization
  void Start()
  {


  }

  // Update is called once per frame
  void Update()
  {
    //every update we subtract delta time. this
    //allows us to count down in seconds
    timer -= Time.deltaTime;
```

```
    //if our timer is up, spawn a new platform
    if (timer < 0f)
    {
        //randomly choose a y value within the
        //right distance to place the new platform
        float yRange = Random.Range(transform.↵
        position.y - placementDistanceRange,↵
        transform.position.y + ↵
        placementDistanceRange);

        //ask our object pool for a platform
        GameObject platform = ObjectPool.instance.↵
        GetObjectFromPool();
        if (platform != null)
        {
            //drop the platform at the correct location
            platform.transform.position = new ↵
            Vector3(transform.position.x, yRange, 0);
            //orient the platform
            platform.transform.rotation = Quaternion.↵
            identity;
            //activate the platform so we can interact
            //with it
            platform.SetActive(true);
        }

        //now that we've placed the platform let's set
        //the duration before spawning a new one
        timer = Random.Range(minimumDropTime,↵
        maximumDropTime);
    }
  }
}
```

To finish things, up we want to add our Spawner and our ObjectPool scripts to our Spawner game object. On the ObjectPool script component we want to drag our Platform Prefab from the project pane into the field called Game Object To Pool. We can also set the number of objects to pool (Figure 7.7). We have ours set to 5, but depending on the object you are pooling, and how fast they are needed, that value should always be adjusted, so only a couple of objects are inactive at any point.

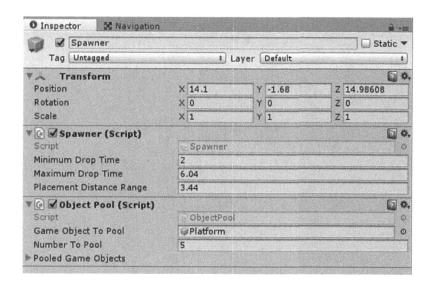

FIGURE 7.7 We can expand the Pooled Game Objects array while the game is running to see our pool function.

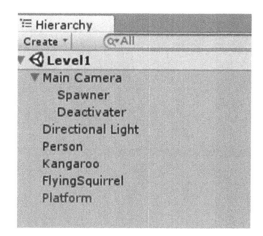

FIGURE 7.8 Our finished hierarchy!

If you want to verify everything is set up correctly this is what the hierarchy should look like in Figure 7.8.

Run the game and you should be able to swap between characters by using the 1, 2, and 3 keys on your keyboard and jump using the spacebar.

CHAPTER 8

Artificial Intelligence (AI) and Non-Player Characters (NPCs)

O KAY, BEFORE YOU GET too excited about this, we're not going to be doing any sort of Turing test passing idea for AI. AI in this context is simple avatars that aren't being controlled by the player—simple enemies and NPCs.

We'll be showing you how to program an enemy that follows a certain patrol route and then reacts when the player comes within a certain distance. In this case, we'll have the enemy chase the player's avatar—but there are plenty of other reactions an AI might have.

We'll be creating an AI using a design pattern called a finite state machine. Finite state machines are a series of states—in this case wander, pursue, and attack—and transitions. The state machine can only be in one state at any given time, and the only way to get from one state to another is via a transition. Transitions only connect one state to another state. And they only go in one direction. So, if we need to have the ability to move from one state and then back, we would need two separate transitions (Figure 8.1).

Different situations can trigger transitions in the state machine so that it moves from one state to another. This allows the finite state machine to react to the game world and operate on its own.

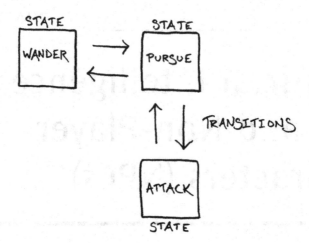

FIGURE 8.1 In the code for this recipe, you will find that our AI has a *wander*, *pursue*, and *attack* state.

PROJECT SETUP

The first thing we'll do to get the AI setup is add all of the relevant actors, and a playfield. Let's start by adding a plane to our hierarchy, naming it "ground," and scaling it to (4, 1, 4).

Now let's add a capsule and name it Player. If you have a player model to use you can insert that instead. Next, add a character controller to our Player. Finally create a new C# script called `PlayerMovement`, and add the following code to it:

```
------------------PlayerMovement.cs------------------

using System.Collections;
using System.Collections.Generic;
using UnityEngine;

public class PlayerMovement : MonoBehaviour
{

  public float speed = 6.0f;
  public float gravity = 15f;
  public float jumpStrength = 10f;

  private CharacterController controller;
  private Vector3 movement = Vector3.zero;
  //this is a shortcut for: new Vector3 (0f, 0f, 0f);
```

```csharp
    private Vector3 movement = Vector3.zero;

    // Use this for initialization
    void Start()
    {
      //we need to get a reference to the character
      //controller component attached to this game object
      controller = GetComponent<CharacterController>();
    }

    // Update is called once per frame
    void Update()
    {

      if (controller.isGrounded)
      {
        //we can apply the forces from the axes to our
        //movement vector
        movement = new Vector3(Input.GetAxis ↵
        ("Horizontal"), 0.0f, Input.GetAxis ↵
        ("Vertical"));
        movement = transform.↵
        TransformDirection(movement);
        movement *= speed;

        if (Input.GetButton("Jump"))
        {
          movement.y = jumpStrength;
        }
      }
      else
      {
        //if we're not on the ground, gravity
        //should pull us down
        movement.y -= gravity * Time.deltaTime;
      }

      //apply the movement vector to our character
      //controller, using delta time to stay consistent
      controller.Move(movement * Time.deltaTime);
    }
}
```

Once you are done, attach the script component to the Player game object. This is a simple script to move a player that can be convenient to use in a wide variety of 3D games. In order to properly test that our AI is working we'll need to move our player in and out of range.

We want to add our enemy now. If you have a model ready to use, you can import and use that. Otherwise, select one of the Unity game objects. We decided to use a sphere, a hovering evil sphere of chasing. Whatever your choice, add your object to the hierarchy. Next add a new character controller to your object; in our case, we added it to our sphere.

We'll want to set up a few waypoints around our level so our AI knows where to patrol. Start by adding a new Empty game object to the hierarchy and naming it Waypoints. Next, add a cube to the hierarchy and name it Waypoint. Next, add the tag *Waypoint* to it and drag it onto the project panel to create a Prefab, then delete the original from your scene. Now add any number of our new waypoint and Prefabs as children under the Waypoints Empty game object, this helps keep them organized. Four is a good number to start with (Figure 8.2). We will want to spread them out slightly, and not have too many obstacles in the way for now since we are testing (Figure 8.3).

Next, create a new C# script called `AIStateMachine`. We will be utilizing inheritance again to keep our code organized and reusable. There won't be much going on in this script, but it will be our base class. This accomplishes a few things. It allows us to have multiple AIs all based off the same template. Any child class that inherits from `AIStateMachine`

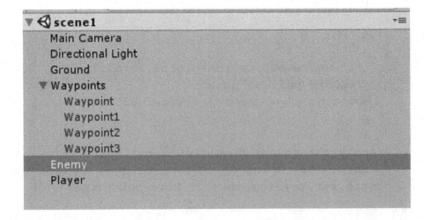

FIGURE 8.2 Collapsing "Waypoints" allows us to keep our hierarchy clean.

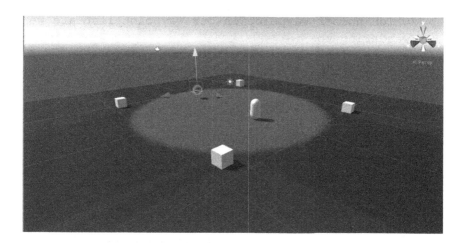

FIGURE 8.3   Our AI is almost ready to chase us.

can have customized behaviors, respond and interact with the player differently, but share the same foundation. This helps us to be more efficient by staying consistent and not starting from scratch each time. If we have any changes or new functionality we need to affect all of our AIs, we can make those changes in the base class and all the child classes will inherit those changes.

Add the following code to `AIStateMachine`.

```
------------------AIStateMachine.cs------------------

using System.Collections;
using System.Collections.Generic;
using UnityEditor;
using UnityEngine;

public class AIStateMachine : MonoBehaviour
{
  //headers allow us to label sections in the inspector
  [Header("From AIStateMachine")]
  //our target will be our player in this case
  public GameObject target;

  //the waypoint list allows our enemy to patrol when it
  //is not chasing the target
  public GameObject[] waypointList;
```

```
//which number waypoint in our waypoint list are we
//wandering to
protected int currentWaypoint;
//the location of our next waypoint
protected Vector3 nextWaypointPosition;
protected CharacterController controller;

// Use this for initialization
void Start()
{
   //we'll have this AI start out at the
   //first waypoint
   currentWaypoint = 0;
   //the AI specific initialization method
   AIinitialization();
}

//the AI specific initialization method is marked
//virtual so child classes can modify it
protected virtual void AIinitialization()
{
   //this is where we'll put any initialization code
   //that all our AIs might need
}

// Update is called once per frame
void Update()
{
   //We'll update the AI tick method to allow the AI
   //to update
   AITick();
}

//the AI specific tick method is marked virtual so
//child classes can modify it
virtual void AITick()
{
   //this is where we'll put any tick code that all
   //our AIs might need
   }
}
```

A number of methods are marked `virtual`. This allows the child classes to override them with their own more specific version of the method. This also allows our child classes to write specific code for that AI, while using the more generalized version in the parent class with the `base` keyword. Take note that we will not need to add this script to any game objects; instead, we will be adding one of its child classes to the game objects.

Now that we have our template, let's develop our AI. Let's create a new C# script called `EnemyAI` and add the following code to it:

```
--------------------EnemyAI.cs------------------------

using System.Collections;
using System.Collections.Generic;
using UnityEngine;


public class EnemyAI : AIStateMachine
{
  //enums let us represent numbers as text. they are
  //words that map to numbers
  public enum AIState
  {
    None = 0,
    Wander = 1,
    Pursue = 2,
    Attack = 3
    //if we add any new states we would need to add
    //to the enum
  }

  //headers allow us to label sections in the
  //inspector
  [Header("From EnemyAI")]
  public float speed = 4.0f;
  //the range where our AI will "see" our character
  public float pursueRange;
  //the range where our AI will attack the player
  public float attackRange;
```

```
//we have a method for printing out debug info. we
//can enable this output by changing this value to
//true in the inspector
public bool printDebugInfo = false;

//we are using this to track our current state
public AIState currentState;

//a reference to the target's transform
//for convenience
private Transform targetPosition;

private Vector3 movement;
private float gravity = 15f;

protected override void AIinitialization()
{
  controller = GetComponent<CharacterController>();

  //let's start out in the wander state
  currentState = AIState.Wander;
  targetPosition = target.transform;
  PrintDebugInfo("Starting out in " + currentState);

  //we have the option to call AIinitialization()
  //in our parent class, uncomment the following line
  //if needed
  base.AIinitialization();
}


//we use our AI tick method to update the
//appropriate state
protected override void AITick()
{
  //if we add any new states we'd need to update
  //this section
  switch (currentState)
```

```
  {
    case AIState.Attack:
      //update attack
      AttackStateUpdate();
      break;

    case AIState.Pursue:
      //update pursue
      PursueStateUpdate();
      break;

    case AIState.Wander:
      //update wander
      WanderStateUpdate();
      break;

    default:
      //if we encounter a state that's not defined
      //throw an error
      Debug.LogError("Unexpected state ↵
      encountered!");
      break;
    }

  //we have the option to call AITick() in our
  //parent class, uncomment the following line if
  //needed
  base.AITick();
}

//this is our pursue state
private void PursueStateUpdate()
{
  //transition from pursue to attack. this triggers
  //when we are closer then the attack range
  if ((Vector3.Distance(transform.position,↵
  targetPosition.position) < attackRange))
```

```
  {
    PrintDebugInfo("Transition: Pursue -> Attack");
    //change the state
    currentState = AIState.Attack;
  }
  //transition from pursue to wander. this triggers
  //when we are farther than the pursue range
  else if (Vector3.Distance(transform.position,↵
  targetPosition.position) > pursueRange)
  {
    PrintDebugInfo("Transition: Pursue -> Wander");
    currentState = AIState.Wander;
  }

  //movement code
  movement = targetPosition.position - transform.↵
  position;
  movement = movement.normalized * speed;

  movement.y -= gravity * Time.deltaTime;

  controller.Move(movement * Time.deltaTime);
}
//this is our attack state
private void AttackStateUpdate()
{
  PrintDebugInfo("ATTACK");

  //movement code
  movement.y -= gravity * Time.deltaTime;

  PrintDebugInfo("Transition: Attack -> Pursue");
  //after attacking once the AI reverts to the
  //pursue state
  currentState = AIState.Pursue;
}

//this is our wander state
private void WanderStateUpdate()
{
  //find the current waypoint
```

```
  Vector3 waypointPosition =↵
  waypointList[currentWaypoint].transform.position;

  //transition from wander to pursue. this triggers
  //when we are within the pursue range
  if (Vector3.Distance(transform.position,↵
    targetPosition.position) < pursueRange)
  {
    PrintDebugInfo("Transition: Wander -> Pursue");
    //change the state
    currentState = AIState.Pursue;
  }

  //movement code
  movement = waypointPosition - transform.position;
  movement = movement.normalized * speed;

  movement.y -= gravity * Time.deltaTime;

  controller.Move(movement * Time.deltaTime);
}

//when we intersect a trigger
private void OnTriggerEnter(Collider other)
{
  //is the object we collided with a waypoint
  if (other.gameObject.CompareTag("Waypoint"))
  {
    //call the NextWaypoint() method to target the
    //next point
    NextWaypoint();
  }
}

//this method is to update the next way point our
//AI is wandering to
private void NextWaypoint()
{
  //add one to the waypoint and use the modulus
  //operator to keep it from going out of bounds
  //if it's out of bounds it will loop back to zero
  //so we will go through all points in order
```

```
        currentWaypoint = (currentWaypoint + 1) % ⏎
        waypointList.Length;
        PrintDebugInfo("Moving to waypoint " + ⏎
        currentWaypoint);
    }

    //this is our method for printing debug info. it
    //takes a string parameter
    private void PrintDebugInfo(string message)
    {
        //if the printDebugInfo field is true we will print
        //debug info. we can toggle this in the inspector
        if (printDebugInfo)
        {
            Debug.Log(message);
        }
    }
}
```

After the script has been completed, add the script component to the Enemy game object. Before we send the enemy on its way, wandering and chasing the poor player, we need to tell it which waypoints it needs to wander between. Set the waypoint list to the same number as the number of waypoints you added to your scene. From there drag all of the waypoints from our hierarchy into each of the locations (Figure 8.4).

Lastly, we need to tell the AI whom to chase. Drag the Player from the hierarchy into the Target field in our EnemyAI script component.

Now we should be able to observe our AI wandering from waypoint-to-waypoint. If we interrupt its wandering by moving into its range we should see it start to pursue us. Once we safely escape, it will return to its wandering. It's a simple AI, one without true pathfinding, but it's an effective technique that's been used in many games (Figure 8.5).

If we want to create a new type of AI, it should inherit from AIStateMachine. We can add our own behaviors and transitions, and have a new creature. These AIs don't always need to be enemies either. Maybe you could change the Attack state to a Celebrate state and we'd have a new friend, looking for us when we come in range.

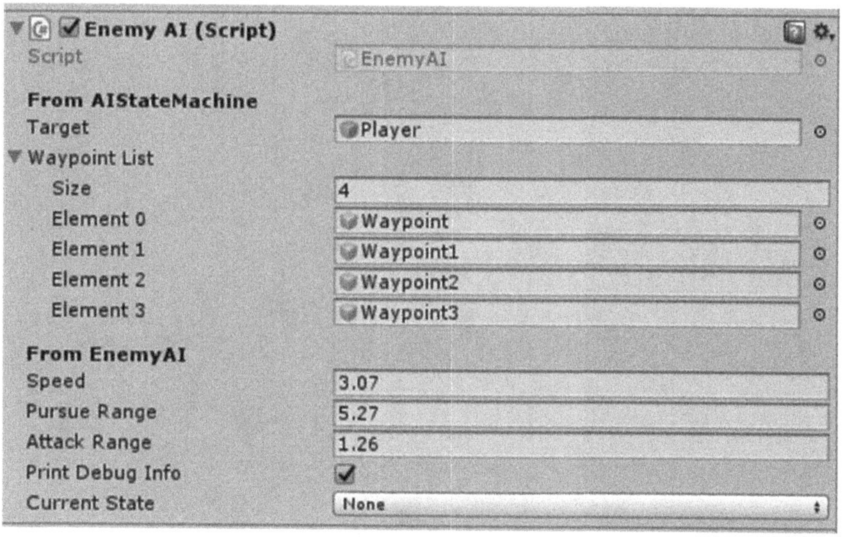

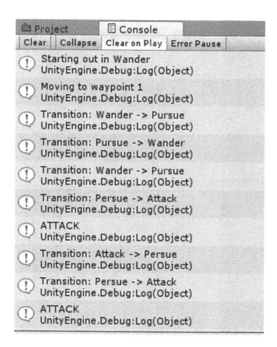

FIGURE 8.4   We can name our waypoints to keep them organized.

FIGURE 8.5   Here we can see the output from our EnemyAI debug messages.

CHAPTER 9

Physics-Based Character Controller

T HE PREVIOUS CHAPTER COVERED creating a character based on a character controller. But such characters aren't able to interact with physics objects. There are ways to fake that interaction—but that would involve additional code for each type of interaction. In this project, you'll learn another way to make characters move through your game.

This chapter explore creating a physics-based character and moving the character using physics forces.

Basing a character on a physics object allows it to interact with any other physics objects in the game scene. We will be creating a character, picking an appropriate collider shape to simulate its interactions, and giving it a rigidbody—which allows it to have mass, drag, and gives our physical forces something to interact with.

In the code, we've created a character called robot friend who is moving around a square space and gathering spheres.

PROJECT SETUP

This is the code recipe where we bring our robot friend to life (Figure 9.1). First, add a plane to our hierarchy, name it "ground," and scale it to (4, 1, 4). Now we want to add our player. We added a simple robot model to our scene hierarchy and named it RobotFriend. If you don't have a robot friend model handy using a cube or capsule will work as well.

FIGURE 9.1   A robot friend! Here to cheer you on!

▼ Constraints			
Freeze Position	☐ X	☐ Y	☐ Z
Freeze Rotation	☑ X	☐ Y	☑ Z

FIGURE 9.2   Freezing the rotation prevents our robot friend from toppling over.

Next, we need to add a RigidBody component to our RobotFriend. The Rigidbody component is responsible for simulating the physical forces: gravity, drag, and giving our game object mass. We want to expand the Constraints section and Freeze Rotation on the X and Z axes (Figure 9.2). Next, we need to add a collider component. If you selected one of Unity's

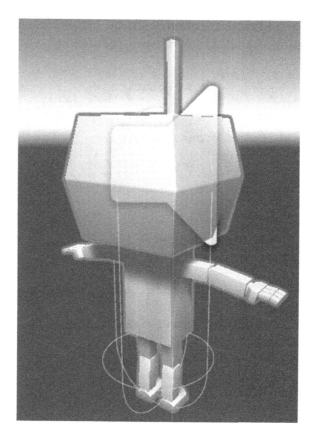

FIGURE 9.3   You'll want your collider to match the shape and be slightly smaller than your object.

game objects, such as a cube, you will probably not need to add a collider component. The specific collider you choose to use is up to you, but you want to keep in mind that it should roughly fit the shape. We selected a Capsule Collider component and added it to our RobotFriend game object (Figure 9.3).

The Capsule Collider (or whichever collider component you selected) is responsible for the shape of the collision. We can make it wider, taller, or narrower and the physics engine will account for the changes you make to the shape. Keep in mind the collider does not need to match the shape of the visual model, but keeping them relatively similar is a best practice.

Now we can add a script to our robot friend. Let's create a new C# script called `MoveRobot` and add the following code to it:

```
--------------------MoveRobot.cs--------------------

using System.Collections;
using System.Collections.Generic;
using UnityEngine;

public class MoveRobot : MonoBehaviour
{
  //the speed for our robot
  public float forwardSpeed = 10f;
  public float rotationSpeed = 80f;

  //we can store a reference to our rigidbody so we
  //can effect it
  private Rigidbody robotRigidBody;

  //used to store the input from our axes
  private float verticalAxis;
  private float horizontalAxis;


  // Use this for initialization
  void Start ()
  {
      //get and store a reference to the rigidbody
      //attached to this game object
      robotRigidBody = GetComponent<Rigidbody>();
  }

  // Update is called once per frame
  void Update ()
  {
      //during the update step, get the
      //horizontal and vertical axes
      verticalAxis = Input.GetAxis("Vertical");
      horizontalAxis = Input.GetAxis ↲
      ("Horizontal");
  }
```

```
//fixed update is the update method specifically
//for physics. it always runs at a predictable rate
//so our physics stay consistent
private void FixedUpdate()
{
    //we create a vector representing our forward
    //movement by using the verticalAxis
    Vector3 forwardMovement = new Vector3(0f, 0f,↵
    forwardSpeed * verticalAxis);
    //we create a vector representing our rotational
    //movement by using the horizontalAxis
    Vector3 rotation = new Vector3(0f, rotationSpeed ↵
    * horizontalAxis);

    //we apply the forward movement vector directly
    //to the rigidbody
    robotRigidBody.AddRelativeForce(forwardMovement);
    //we apply the rotational movement directly to
    //the rigidbody
    robotRigidBody.AddRelativeTorque(rotation);

    //if our robot is moving faster than the
    //maximum speed
    if (robotRigidBody.velocity.magnitude >
    forwardSpeed)
    {
      //this slows down to the max speed
      robotRigidBody.velocity = robotRigidBody.
      velocity.normalized * forwardSpeed;
    }
  }
}
```

Now add the MoveRobot script to the RobotFriend game object. We can edit the forwardSpeed and the rotationSpeed fields on the script component along with the Mass, Drag, and Angular Drag on our Rigidbody component to change how the robot moves and feels. The important thing to remember is this is all done with physics.

Now in order to play around with our RobotFriend a bit more let's add a sphere to our hierarchy and add a rigidbody component to it (Figure 9.4).

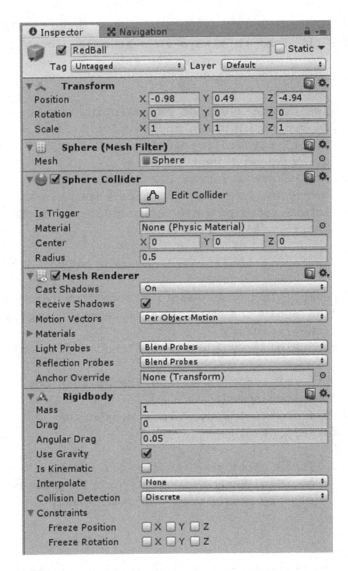

FIGURE 9.4   Adding a rigidbody allows robot friend and the sphere to interact using physics.

Duplicate this sphere as many times as you'd like and try playing the game again (Figure 9.5). Now we're able to interact directly with physics objects, unlike using a CharacterController component. We can use these tools to create the basics of a physics-based game. You can also add walls so RobotFriend does not fall into the abyss, this is what our hierarchy looks like (Figure 9.6). Now we're able to interact directly with physics objects.

FIGURE 9.5   A screenshot of our "game."

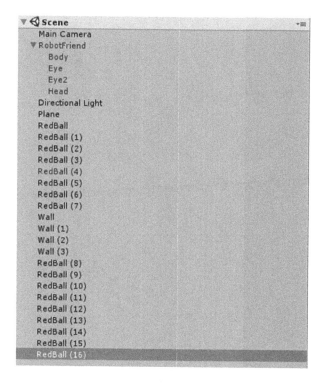

FIGURE 9.6   Your hierarchy with all your game objects.

Appendix: Other Tools and Not Reinventing the Wheel

B Y NOW YOU ARE hopefully more confident when it comes to basic programming concepts than when you started. You have the tools to start working in Unity, to create, explore, and make games. But! The landscape of tools—especially free or low-cost tools—available to game developers is changing and improving all the time.

Depending on what sort of games you're interested in making—you may want to look at these as you are getting started.

What you've learned in this book won't necessarily be directly applicable to these programs—but one of the things we've looked at how a computer thinks. This will let you be more effective and creative with the following tools.

Hanna spent a lot of time basically trying to figure out how to make Twine, so that she could make a game. After a year flailing against technical difficulties, someone showed her Twine. Don't wait for that. Look for the right tool for the job.

STORY TOOLS

One of the things we discovered when we got into writing this book was that a lot of artists were interested in making story games or role-playing games. If your goal is to focus more on writing a story than writing a program, then there are a lot of tools at your disposal. Below we'll look at a handful of them.

There are a variety of story tools—many wonderful ones—and all of them cater to slightly different levels of programming and game design experience. If you are interested in storytelling—and/or have a lot of time in your hands—check out as many as you can find. Below you'll find a few to get you started. But there are more out there. And between the time that we write this book and the time it's published, there will be more still. Good luck!

Twine

twinery.org

Twine is a free tool built for writers without programming experience to make story games. Twine is great. The format and interface lends itself to building story webs and it's easy to use. If you are trying to write a story with game-like elements, then go play with Twine. Actually, probably go play with Twine at some point anyway.

Twine stories are laid out like a mind map or a wiki—each story bit can lead to many other story bits. You'll need to use the language built for Twine, but it was designed from the get go to be simple and friendly to nonprogrammers.

Twine was built and is maintained for free. But you can donate to the good fellow who built it.

Inkle Writer

www.inklestudios.com/inklewriter

Its interface is friendly to non-programmers. The author of the game writes snippets of text followed by options—very much like an old *Choose Your Own Adventure* book. It doesn't have the built in flexibility that Twine does, but it's a great structure.

You can also start writing in Inklewriter for free!

RPG Maker

www.rpgmakerweb.com

Are you actually, secretly making an RPG? Do you have a team to work with? No? Then you should be using this, or something like it, and not trying to program it yourself. It is what the name implies and you'll save yourself a lot of time, trouble, and heartache by starting here.

RPG Maker MV will set you back about $80, but it's now available on for Mac and PC.

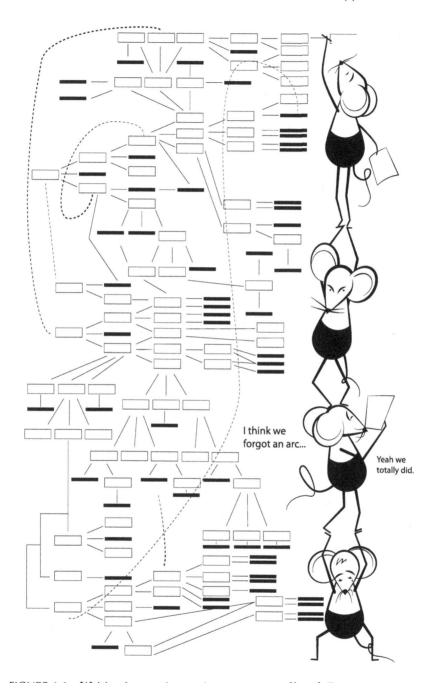

FIGURE A.1 Writing interactive stories can get out of hand. Fast.

A Few More

Other story game tools include Texture, Inform, and ChoiceScript. If you are narrative focused, there a lot of interesting and useful tools at your disposal. Consider using a tool that's designed for storytelling. If you want something that combines storytelling with the Unity skills you've learned, look into Yarn and YarnSpinner.

OTHER TOOLS

Maybe you have a more abstract concept for your game. Or maybe, as much as learning to programming is awesome ('cause it is, right?) there is likely a piece of software out there that's a better fit for what you want to do. So, here are a few more tools to check out, if you aren't sure that programming from scratch is what right for you.

Processing

Processing is a tool designed for prototyping and to teach programming—especially for those who come from a visual arts background. Sounds pretty cool, right? It is. The syntax is similar to what we used in this book, so you shouldn't have trouble getting started.

GameMaker

It's a lovely program, free, and designed to make interactive digital art. Might just be what you're looking for.

We talked about GameMaker in chapter two, but we wanted to remind you about it here. GameMaker is a program designed to let you make 2D games without coding. It's got a drag-and-drop interface that's easy to follow. If you want to get more complex, then you can add your own code too! This tool uses GML (Game Maker Language—its own programming language), which is similar enough to the languages we've talked about that you should be able to get started.

While the basics of GameMaker are pretty simple, it's been used to make games like Spelunky, Undertale, and Hyper Light Drifter. It might be a good tool to investigate—letting you blend your new coding skills but still produce something playable in a short period of time.

Acknowledgments

W E WOULD LIKE TO express our thanks to our agent Jennifer Chen Tran, to our editors Rick Adams and Jessica Vega, and to all the folks at CRC Press/Taylor & Francis Group. Books are never the work of one person and y'all did a fantastic job. We'd also like to thank Stephanie Frankiewicz for her beautiful illustrations! (She did the good ones!)

We'd like to thank everyone who talked to us about the project and shared their thoughts and experiences as artists and creatives, especially Wesley Adams, Robert, Lizzie Wise, Tabby Rose, Brian Crick, Jacinta, Tommy Sunders, Jenny Slife, Alyssa Herman, Ethan, Jillian Stiles, Mike Sill, Michael Swearingen, Christopher Khuong, Chris Sanyk, Zed, Evan Edwards, Jasmine Burks, Michael Beyene, Laura Garabedian, Natilya Ratcliff, Jake Pierce, Ryan Krause, Sean Hinchee, Alex, Colin Wolfe, Karl I. Polley, Tanner Tiffany, and Quinlan Omahne.

Jarryd

Wow! It's here! I never thought I'd ever write a book, much less have one published. I'd like to thank a few of the people without whom this would not be possible. First, thanks to my coauthor, Hanna, who encouraged and helped a scared Jarryd write the original proposal. It's been quite the adventure and I'm thankful to have gone through it together.

Thanks to Bill Whetsel George Kopec for having me as a guest on the North Coast Game Educators Alliance podcast. The conversations there planted the seed that became this book. Thank you for continuing to inspire me. Next I thank Chris Totten, who originally pushed me to pursue authorship and performed the introduction that made this possible. Thank you so much to my Cleveland Game Developers family!—Matt Perrin, Stephanie Frankiewicz, Justin Demetroff, Steve Felix, Sam Marcus, Brian Crick, Chris Sanyk, Joe O'Rourke, Eagan Rackley, and every single member of the group. This group has helped me grow in countless ways and I'm so very thankful.

In no particular order, I thank Eric Schneider, Nele Custers, Suzanne Jackiw, Nixie Pixel, Michael Sill, Chris Deleon, Tabby and Jeff Rose, Catt Small, Brandon Sheffield, Shawn Alexander Allen, and all of my game dev fam. Last but not least, I thank my family: my wonderful in-laws and extended family; my siblings for always being there and for the movie quotes; mom for always believing in me; my son, Lancelot, for being my daily joy; and my wife, Mikayla, for being my sanity, my best friend, and my biggest supporter. I love you! And to God.

p.s. If I forgot your name I'M SO SORRY! D: Write it here._____
THANKS!

Hanna

If my life depended on it, I would never have guessed that the first published book I had a hand in writing would be nonfiction and about game programming. So, many thanks to my coauthor, Jarryd. This has been a fascinating process and I've come out the other side of it with a dear friend, for which I'm grateful.

Chelsea, there are a lot of things I wouldn't have done without you, and working in games is one of them; therefore, so is this book. Thanks to my writing crew: Jae, Cole, Brad, and Clarice. You've all put up with my nonsense at one point or another when it comes to pursuing the art of putting one word after another and in life in general.

Thanks to my parents and in-laws, for believing in me and supporting me. Thanks to all the mentors and friends who've been a part of this project—both directly and indirectly. Leah, you are a wonder—thanks for the serious conversations and simple encouragement throughout this process. All my love and thanks to Eamonn, for being an extremely understanding 9-year-old, to Touchstone, for sitting with me through writing and edits, and—of course—to Damian, the love of my life, with gusto.

A (Mostly Serious) Basic Game Jargon Glossary

avatar: a visual representation of the player or user in a digital environment. Most frequently in games—the visual that represents the Player Character

balancing: tweaking and polishing the game's rules, so that they fair and/or engaging. This can refer to a number of things: balancing an in-game economy, a character's ability to jump, and lots of other systems in the game. Balancing is making it better

boss: a powerful enemy in a video game, usually the final fight for a level, a section of a game, or an entire game

bug: something that has gone wrong and needs to be fixed in the code. One must squash all the bugs one can find

console: a console is a piece of hardware designed to play games on. An Xbox or PlayStation would be examples of game consoles. Most games designed for a console also work on a PC

downloadable content (DLC): an expansion of some type for a game. It's released after the game, and is an augment or extension of the game. Examples would be new skins, new story content, extra levels, etc.

experience points or XP: a common way of tracking a player's progress through a game. Experience Points are accumulated by completing tasks in the game and generally when a certain number of XP is collected the player will level up

first person shooter (FPS): a game played from a first person perspective—as though we are seeing the world through the character's eyes—with a shooting mechanic. If someone is complaining about violence in video games, they are probably thinking of First Person Shooters

first person/third person: these are perspectives in video games. In first person we see through the character's eyes. In third person we usually see over their shoulder or from slightly behind them

free to play (F2P): a game that is free to download or install, but usually offers in-app purchases. Generally makes its money from very small purchases called microtransactions

indie game: a game made by individuals—or small to medium sized teams—and/or without the funding of a large company or publisher. Such folks can be called indie game developers or indies

head-up display (HUD): a visual representation of information to the player, displayed as part of the user interface but not necessarily a part of the game world. Whenever you have something that tells you how much time you have left, how many lives you have left, a mini map—all that is part of the HUD

massive multiplayer online (MMO): an online game that can support a large number of players. World of Warcraft. See also, a Time Sink

mechanic: A simple definition for a game mechanic is tricky, but here's our try: a component or system in your game that allows for interaction. A part of the game being used (or interacted with) according to the game rules. Examples might be a roll of the dice in a board game, or a jump in a video game

mobile: generally, mobile is going to be referring to a mobile platform: so a mobile device you can play games on: a phone, a tablet, etc.

nonplayer character (NPC): all the characters in a game that the player does not control. Usually NPC refers to a character that's a part (even a very small one) of the game's story

platform: the hardware that a game is played on. See Mobile, Console, and PC^2

platformer: a kind of game where players jump from platform-to-platform. Usually 2D. Usually with obstacles

player versus player (PvP): a game, or a part of a game, where players play against each other. Also known as "experiences designed to test the limits of friendship and other important relationships"

player character (PC^1): the character the player controls!

personal computer (PC^2): a Personal Computer

role-playing game (RPG): in the context of video games: a game where the player plays as a character or group of character, usually story heavy. These games tend to be played in third person — looking over the character's shoulder

sandbox: a game with a relatively open world and without the strong imposition of a linear goal. A sandbox world in a game is one you can play around in, rather than needing to go from point A to point B

side scroller: a type of game that scrolls sideways, it's a 2D game where we see the characters from the side and they move across the screen (usually from left to right) in order to reach the end of the level

time sink: we just put this definition in here so we could refer to it in the MMO definition. But since we're here, let's say it's a game that you can pour many hours into. A decent percentage of your life even, if you so choose

tower defense: a kind of strategy game where one defends a certain location against AI or human enemies, which is generally accomplished by placing defensive or offensive structures around that location

triple A (AAA): a term for big budget games made by large studios

twitter: where game devs hide online

user experience (UX): the experience of the player playing your game. Not to be taken lightly or for granted…ever

user interface (UI): the means by which the player interacts with your game—both what they see on the screen and the objects they use to interact with that screen (a mouse, a keyboard, etc.)

Index

Printed in the United States
by Baker & Taylor Publisher Services